Nita Mehta's
Different ways with
Paneer

Nita Mehta's
Different ways with
Paneer

Nita Mehta

M.Sc. (Food and Nutrition), Gold Medalist

Tanya Mehta

SNAB
Publishers Pvt. Ltd.

Nita Mehta's
Different ways with
Paneer

© Copyright 2003 **SNAB** Publishers Pvt Ltd

First Hardbound Edition 2003

ISBN 81-7869-050-0

Food Styling & Photography: **SNAB**

Layout and laser typesetting:

National Information Technology Academy
3A/3, Asaf Ali Road
New Delhi-110002
N.I.T.A. ☎ 23252948

Picture on page 1:	**Kalyani Paneer** **Mewa Seekh in Gravy** **Stuffed Khubani in Syrup**
Picture on page 2:	**Pina Cheese Cake**
Picture on last page:	**Hyderabadi Dum Biryani** **Vegetable Seekh**
Picture on back cover:	**Achaari Paneer Cigars** **Hara Bhara Kebab**

Published by:

SNAB
Publishers Pvt Ltd
3A/3 Asaf Ali Road
New Delhi-110002

The Best of Cookery Books

Editorial and Marketing office:
E-348, Greater Kailash-II, N.Delhi-48
Fax: 91-11-26235218 *Tel:* 91-11-26214011, 26238727
E-Mail: nitamehta@email.com
snab@snabindia.com

Website: http://www.nitamehta.com
Website: http://www.snabindia.com

Printed at:
INTERNATIONAL PRINT-O-PAC LIMITED

Distributed by:
THE VARIETY BOOK DEPOT
A.V.G. Bhavan, M 3 Con Circus
New Delhi - 110 001
Tel: 23417175, 23412567; Fax: 23415335

Price: Rs. 245/-

INTRODUCTION

In every home, paneer is the queen of dishes. A rich source of protein, paneer is very versatile. Paneer is used with many vegetables to create nutritious and well balanced meals. Besides being used for Indian delights, it can be very deliciously used in Continental, Chinese and Thai dishes. This book offers *Garlic Honey Paneer, Green Thai Paneer Curry, Cottage Cheese Florentine* and many other wonderful dishes. In the recipe *"Iman Binalde"* paneer is very successfully combined with chick-peas (kabuli chaanas). The dish is then baked to produce a Continental delight. Tofu is substituted with the easily available paneer in noodles for the Chinese food lovers. The Indian delights include *Hyderabadi Paneer Biryani* and delicious paneer parathas flavoured with carom seeds.

There are snacks which can be served as starters before a meal and many tea time snacks for the evenings. The ever-green *Paneer Tikka* and other tandoori snacks are very simple to make once you follow the recipes step by step. The pictures of the steps will make the job very simple. A few snacky meals like *Cheesey Broccoli Wraps, Chilli Paneer Dosa,* are new creations for evenings. When you do not feel like cooking a regular meal, give your family these delicious snacky meals.

The last section of sweet has Continental *Cheese cakes* prepared with paneer paste instead of the foreign ricotta cheese. *Khubani Stuffed with grated paneer in Kewra Syrup* is sure to fascinate the Indian palate.

With this book besides you, surprise your friends with creations they will not anticipate. Use this book for a variety of new paneer dishes for your parties and family get togethers.

Enjoy!

Nita Mehta

Contents

Tea Time & Snacky Meals   32

Indian Meal Time Dishes

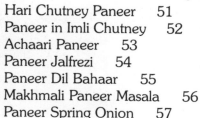

Dry & Masala　　48

Indian Meal Time Dishes

Gravies & Curries　　64

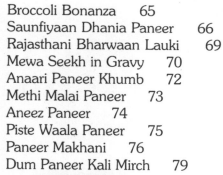

Chinese & Thai　　91

Continental   99

Noodles, Rice & Roti   109

The Sweet Touch   120

Starters

- The most delicious snack in the world can fail to tempt if it is presented in an unbecoming manner! A greasy or too oily snack is no more appetizing, so make it a habit to remove the fried snack from oil on a tissue or a paper napkin to absorb the excess oil.

- A few crisp leaves of lettuce or a sprig of mint or coriander placed at the edge of the serving platter makes the snack irresistible! Make the green leaves crisp by putting them in a bowl of cold water and keeping them in the fridge for 3-4 hours or even overnight. Some cucumber slices or tomato wedges placed along with the greens, beautify it further.

- A teaspoon of til (sesame seeds) or khus-khus (poppy seeds) or ajwain (carom seeds), added to coating mixture or bread crumbs makes the snack interesting.

- For getting a crisp coating on cutlets or rolls, dip prepared snack in a thin batter of maida and water and then roll in bread crumbs. Fry till well browned.

- In the absence of bread crumbs, a mixture of ¼ cup maida and ½ cup suji may be used to get a crisp coating.

- If your cutlets fall apart, quickly tear 1-2 slices of bread and grind in a mixer to get fresh bread crumbs. Add it to the cutlet mixture for binding.

- To make crisp potato chips, soak them in cold water for 1 hour. Drain. Wipe dry and sprinkle some maida (plain flour) on them before frying.

- Never start frying in smoking hot oil as it will turn the snack black. Never fry in cold oil also as the snack may fall apart or it may soak a lot of oil.

- For deep frying any snack, add small quantities to the oil at one time. This maintains the oil's temperature. If too many pieces are added together, the oil turns cold and a lot of oil is then absorbed by the snack.

- After deep frying, let the oil cool down. Add a little quantity of fresh oil to the used oil before reusing. This prevents the oil from discolouring.

Kalyani Paneer

Beautiful rounds of paneer filled with a delicious filling. The leftover paneer could be used for various recipes like lachhedar paneer crisps, mewa seekh in gravy or for delicious paneer kheer etc. ...so don't be worried about the wastage of paneer. Go ahead!

Picture on page 1   Makes 8 -10 pieces

500 gm paneer (take a big block or a single piece weighing 500 gms)

FILLING

**1 potato - boiled and grated finely, 1 tbsp very finely chopped coriander
½ tsp salt or to taste, ½ tsp bhuna jeera, ½ tsp garam masala, ¼ tsp red chilli pd.
1½ tbsp very finely chopped mixed nuts (badam, pista, kishmish etc.)
8- 10 whole badaam (almonds)**

COATING

¼ cup maida, ½ tsp salt, ½ tsp pepper, ½ tsp chaat masala

Step 1

1. Cut paneer into 1" thick slices lengthwise. Cut each slice into rounds of about 1½" diameter with a small sharp lid or a cover of any small round container. This way you get small, thick paneer rounds.

2. In each round, with the help of a scooper or knife make a shallow hole, about ½" deep in the centre, leaving ¼" wall all around. Go a little deep and not too wide. Leave the bottom intact to fill the filling.

Step 2

3. Sprinkle some chaat masala on hollow paneer circles.

4. For filling, boil a potato, peel and grate very finely.

5. Mix all the ingredients of the filling with the potatoes. Check seasonings, mix well.

6. Make very tiny balls of the mixture that would fit into the scooped out hollow of paneer. Place the ball over the paneer hole and press gently to flatten a little. Let the potato topping cover some of the sides of the paneer hole, making the edges of the hole neat.

Step 6

7. Press one whole piece of badam on the filling in the rounds. Press gently so that it sticks in the centre.

8. Mix all the coating ingredients and spread in large flat plate. Coat the paneer circles in it, turning to coat all sides of the paneer and the filling.

9. Heat oil in a kadahi and deep fry the circles till golden brown. Drain on paper napkins. Serve hot.

Jalapeno & Cheese Croquettes

Jalapenos are pronounced as hale- pea- noz, 'j' being pronounced as 'h'. Quick and delicious croquettes taste even better with the cheesy dip given below.. Must give it a try.

Makes 8 croquettes   *Picture on page 50*

125 gms mozzarella cheese- grated (1¼ cups)
100 gm paneer - grated (1 cup)
½ tsp black pepper powder, ½ salt, or to taste, oil for frying
1 slice of bread - churned in a mixer to get fresh bread crumbs
3 jalapenos - chopped finely
or
2 regular green chillies - deseeded, chopped and pickled (soak in 3 tbsp vinegar with ½ tsp salt and 1 tsp sugar for 20 minutes and strain and use)
½ cup maida and 1 cup dry bread crumbs - to coat

Step 2

1. Tear bread into pieces and churn in a mixer to get fresh crumbs.
2. Mix grated paneer, cheese, jalapenos or chillies, pepper, salt and bread crumbs.
3. Divide the mixture into 8 equal portions. Shape each portion into a ball.

Step 4

4. Shape each ball into a big roll, about 2" long. Flatten the sides of the roll, by pressing the sides of the roll against a flat surface. Keep aside.

Step 5

5. Spread maida and bread crumbs in separate flat plates. Take 1 cup of water separately in a shallow flat bowl (katori). Roll croquettes over maida. Then dip the croquette in the water for a second and then immediately roll it over the dry bread crumbs. All the sides should be completely covered with bread crumbs.
6. Heat oil in a kadhai and fry 2 croquettes at a time till golden brown. Serve with dip.

Cheesy Yogurt Dip

½ cup curd - hang for ½ hour in a muslin cloth, ¼ tsp oregano
3 tbsp cheese spread, 1 tbsp milk, ¼ tsp salt, ¼ tsp pepper, ¼ tsp red chilli flakes

1. Mix all together till smooth. Serve with croquettes or any chips, etc.

Lachhedar Paneer Crisps

An extremely crisp snack coated with thin vermicelli (seviyaan).

Picture on page 67   *Makes 12- 14*

2½ cups grated paneer (250 gms)
3 slices bread - churned in a mixer to get fresh bread crumbs
½ cup chopped coriander, ¾ tsp chaat masala
½ tsp bhuna jeera (roasted cumin), ¾ tsp salt, ½ tsp pepper

FILLING
¼ cup channa dal - soaked for 2 hours & ground coarsely without water in a mixer
1 onion - chopped finely, 1 tsp ginger - chopped finely
1 tbsp kaju - chopped, 2 tbsp kishmish - chopped, 1 tbsp oil
¼ tsp haldi, ½ tsp salt, ¼ tsp red chilli powder, ¼ tsp amchoor, ½ tsp garam masala

TO COAT
½ cup very thin seviyaan- roughly broken into small pieces by hand

1. Strain dal and roughly grind in a mixer to a coarse thick paste. Do not grind too much and make it thin and smooth.
2. Heat oil. Add onion, ginger, kaju and kishmish. Cook till onions turn light golden.
3. Add ground dal, haldi, salt, red chilli powder, amchoor and garam masala. Stir for 1-2 minutes. Remove from fire and keep aside.

Step 5

4. Mix grated paneer with coriander, chaat masala, fresh bread crumbs, bhuna jeera, salt and pepper.
5. With a ball of the paneer mixture, make a 2" long oval roll. Flatten it to get a slight depression in the centre. Place 1 tsp of the filling in it along the length. Pick up the sides to cover the filling, such that the filling is completely covered on all sides with the paneer mixture. Shape to give a neat roll with slightly flattened ends.

Step 6

6. Break seviyaan into 1-1½" small pieces. Spread on a plate. Take 1 cup of water separately in a shallow flat bowl (katori). Dip the roll in the water for a second and then immediately roll it over the seviyaan. All the sides should be completely covered with seviyaan.
7. Keep aside to set for 15 minutes. Deep fry 2-3 pieces at a time. Serve with poodina chutney .

Achaari Paneer Cigars

Makes 28 pieces　　　　*Picture on back cover*

DOUGH
1 cup maida (plain flour), 1 tbsp oil, ½ tsp salt, a pinch of baking powder

FILLING
2 cups mashed paneer (200-250 gm)
¼ cup chopped coriander, 1 onion - very finely chopped
1 green chilli - deseeded & chopped, 2 tbsp oil, 1 tsp saunf
½ tsp rai, ½ tsp jeera (cumin seeds), ¼ tsp haldi
½ tsp garam masala, ¾ tsp salt or to taste, ½ tsp red chilli powder
1 tbsp lemon juice or to taste

COATING
1 tbsp til (sesame seeds), 6 tbsp dry bread crumbs, a pinch of orange colour

MAIDA PASTE (MIX TOGETHER)
¼ cup maida (plain flour), ¾ cup water, ¼ tsp salt & ¼ tsp pepper

1. Mix maida, oil, baking powder and salt. Add enough water to make a firm dough. Cover and keep the dough aside for 20-30 minutes.
2. For filling, heat oil. Add saunf, jeera & rai. Wait for 1 minute. Add onions, stir till soft. Add haldi, chilli powder, garam masala & salt. Add paneer & cook on moderate heat till dry. Add coriander & green chillies. Add lemon juice & cook for 1 minute. Remove from fire & keep aside.
3. Make very thin chappatis, each as big as the chakla (8"-9" diameter) on low heat on a tawa, keeping it white. Remove from tawa. Keep soft in a casserole.
4. Cut each chappati into 4 pieces to get 4 triangular pieces. On each piece put 1½ tbsp of filling, 1" away from the pointed end and roll up to cover filling.
5. Fold the right and left side a little to enclose the filling & holding the folded sides firmly, roll up to get a cigar shaped roll. Seal the end with a little maida paste. Keep it on a flat surface with the joint side down.
6. Mix bread crumbs with til and colour in a bowl. Spread only 2 tbsp on a plate. Dip each roll in maida batter and then press over bread crumbs. Keep aside, covered with cling film till serving firm.
7. To serve, deep fry till crisp. Serve plain or with any chutney.

Step 4

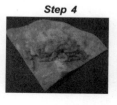
Step 4

Step 4

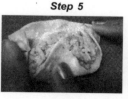
Step 5

Mewa Rolls

Extremely soft and delicious rolls. Make extra as they are usually eaten more than expected, especially at parties.

Makes 20-22

2 cups grated paneer (200 gms)
2 tsp magaz (melon seeds) & 1 tbsp chironji (sunflower seeds) - dry roast on a tawa
a few toothpicks
½ cup dry bread crumbs, see note
1 tbsp cornflour
½ tsp garam masala, ½ tsp salt

GRIND TOGETHER TO A SMOOTH PASTE
¼ tsp jaiphal (nutmeg), ¼ tsp javetri (mace)
10 kaju (cashewnuts), 8 badam (almonds)
5 kishmish (raisins), 5- 6 whole pistas (pistachio)
2 green chillies, ¼ cup green coriander
1" piece ginger, 6-8 flakes garlic

Step 1

1. Roast magaz and chironji on a hot tawa. Cool.
2. Grind all ingredients given under paste in a mixer with 3 tbsp water till smooth.
3. Mix grated paneer, roasted chironji, magaz, bread crumbs, cornflour, garam masala, salt and the prepared paste. Mix well.
4. Take a lemon sized ball of the mixture. Make a small roll of 1½" length. Flatten it from the sides.

Step 5

5. Insert a toothpick from one end coming out a little on the other end, going along the length, without puncturing the roll at any other point. Repeat with the left over mixture. Keep the sticks covered with a cling wrap in the refrigerator for atleast 1 hour.
6. Heat oil in a kadhai. Deep fry the rolls with the toothpicks till golden brown. Drain on napkins. Serve the rolls with the toothpicks.

Note: Store dry bread crumbs in an air tight container in the refrigerator. Dry crumbs are available in the market. To make them at home: Tear 3 bread slices into small pieces and spread in a microproof plate/dish. Micro high for 2 minutes. Mix with hands to change sides and again micro high for 1 minute. Remove from microwave and let it stand for 15 minutes or till dry. Grind in a mixer.

Vegetable Seekh

Makes 15

Picture on page 127

½ cup mashed paneer
1 cup saboot masoor ki dal
1" piece ginger, 8-10 flakes garlic
1 green chilli - chopped, 1 tsp jeera (cumin seeds)
2 laung and seeds of 2 chhoti illaichi - powdered
3 tbsp cornflour
1¼ tsp salt or to taste, 1 tsp garam masala
1 tsp red chilli powder, ¼ tsp amchoor
½ piece of a bread - churn in a mixer to get fresh bread crumbs
2½ tsp lemon juice, 3- 4 tbsp oil
3 tbsp capsicum - chopped, 3 tbsp onion- chopped
2 tbsp tomato (without pulp)- finely chopped

Step 5

1. Soak saboot masoor dal for 2 hours. Strain.
2. Grind dal, ginger, garlic, green chilli and jeera to a thick smooth paste using the minimum amount of water. Keep dal paste aside.
3. Heat 3 tbsp oil in a heavy bottomed kadhai. Add dal. Stir-fry for 4-5 minutes on low flame till dal is dry and does not stick to the bottom of the kadhai. Remove.

Step 6

4. Mix powdered illaichi and laung, cornflour, paneer, salt, garam masala, red chilli powder, amchoor and bread crumbs with the dal. Add lemon juice, 2 tbsp of chopped capsicum, 2 tbsp of chopped onion, 1 tbsp of chopped tomato. Reserve the rest. Mix well. Make balls out of the mixture. Keep aside.
5. Take a ball of dal paste & make a 2" long kebab.
6. Take a pencil or a skewer and push it from one end of the kebab to the other without puncturing at any point.

Step 7

7. Stick remaining chopped onion, capsicum and tomatoes (without pulp) on kebab by pressing vegetables with the palm on to the kebab.
8. Gently pull out the skewer or a pencil.
9. Shallow fry the seekh in medium hot oil on a pan to a light brown colour. Serve hot with chutney.

Mazedaar Balls

Makes 12

1 cup grated broccoli or cauliflower (about ½ of a medium cauliflower)
1 small boiled potato - grated
100 gms of paneer - grated (1 cup)
½ tsp jeera (cumin seeds)
¼" piece ginger - chopped finely
¾ tsp salt or to taste, ¼ tsp red chilli powder
½ tsp garam masala, ¼ tsp amchoor
2 tbsp kaju (cashewnuts) - chopped
1 tbsp kishmish (raisins) - chopped

TOPPING
3 tbsp besan (gram flour)
a pinch of orange colour
a pinch of salt and ajwain (carom seeds)

1. Grate cauliflower or broccoli finely.
2. Heat 1½ tbsp oil in a kadhai. Add jeera. When jeera turns golden, add ginger. Reduce heat. Saute for ½ minute.
3. Add salt, red chilli powder, garam masala and amchoor.
4. Add cashewnuts and raisins. Stir for a few seconds.
5. Add potatoes. Cook for a minute.
6. Add grated broccoli or cauliflower. Cook for 2 minutes. Remove from fire.
7. Add grated paneer. Mix lightly, do not mash paneer.
8. Make small balls with the mixture.
9. Take out besan in a plate. Add a pinch of orange colour, salt and ajwain.
10. Roll the balls on the besan to coat on all the sides.
11. Heat oil in a kadhai and deep fry the balls 1-2 balls at a time till golden.
12. Serve hot.

Step 1   *Step 8*   *Step 10*

Hara Bhara Kebab

1 cup channe ki dal (split Bengal gram)
1 bundle (600 gm) spinach - discard stems, chop only leaves very finely
3 tbsp oil
3 slices bread - torn into pieces and churned in a mixer to get fresh crumbs
2 tbsp cornflour
2 green chillies - chopped finely
½ tsp red chilli powder, ½ tsp garam masala
¾ tsp salt or to taste, ½ tsp amchoor (dried mango powder)

CRUSH TOGETHER
½ tsp jeera (cumin seeds), seeds of 2 moti illaichi (black cardamom)
3-4 saboot kali mirch (peppercorns), 2-3 laung (cloves)

FILLING
¾ cup grated paneer (75 gms)
1 tbsp chopped coriander, salt and bhuna jeera to taste

1. Crush jeera, seeds of moti illaichi, saboot kali mirch and laung together.
2. Clean, wash dal. Pressure cook dal with the above crushed spices, ½ tsp salt and 2 cups water. After the first whistle, keep the cooker on slow fire for 15 minutes. Remove from fire and keep aside.
3. After the pressure drops down, mash the hot dal with a karchhi. If there is any water, mash the dal on fire and dry the dal as well while you are mashing it. Remove from fire.
4. Discard stem of spinach and chop leaves very finely. Wash in several changes of water. Leave the chopped spinach in the strainer for 15 minutes so that the water drains out.
5. Heat 3 tbsp oil in a kadhai and saute spinach leaves for 8-10 minutes till absolutely dry and well fried.
5. Add fresh bread crumbs, cornflour, spinach, green chillies, salt and masalas to the mashed dal. Make small balls.
6. Mix paneer with coriander, salt and jeera. Flatten spinach-dal balls and put 1 tbsp paneer filling. Cover the filling and form a flattened tikki.
7. Cook them on a non stick pan or a tawa with just 2-3 tbsp oil till brown on both sides. When done shift them on the sides of the tawa so that they turn crisp and the oil drains out while more kebabs can be added to the hot oil in the center of the tawa. Remove the kebabs on paper napkins and serve hot with hari chutney.

Curry Patta Toasties

Picture on page 20   *Serves 4*

75 gm paneer - crumbled or mashed roughly (¾ cup)
2 tbsp suji (semolina)
½ tsp salt, or to taste, ¼ tsp pepper, or to taste
½ onion - very finely chopped
½ tomato - cut into half, deseeded and chopped finely
2 tbsp curry leaves, 3 bread slices - toasted
¼ - ½ tsp rai (small brown mustard seeds), 3 tsp oil to shallow fry

1. Mix the suji, salt and pepper with the paneer using your fingers.
2. Add the onion, tomato and curry leaves.
3. Spread this mixture carefully on the toasted bread slices, keeping the edges neat.
4. Sprinkle some rai over the mixture, pressing down carefully with your finger tips.
5. Heat 1 tsp oil in a pan. Add a slice of bread with the topping side down.
6. Cook until it turns golden brown and crisp. Add a little more oil for the next slice if required. Cut into 8 triangular pieces and serve hot.

Note: This recipe will work best using a minimum quantity of oil for frying.

Mushroom Cheese Discs

Makes 12 - 15

125 gms mushrooms - chopped
250 gm paneer - grated (2½ cups)
2 onions - chopped, 4 flakes of garlic - crushed
3 tbsp chopped parsley or coriander
1 tbsp vinegar, 1 tbsp cornflour
4 - 5 tbsp of dry breadcrumbs, ¾ tsp pepper, 1 salt, or to taste
½ cup maida to coat

Step 2

1. Heat 2 tbsp oil. Add garlic and onion. Cook till onions turn light golden.
2. Add chopped mushrooms, cook on high flame till dry and golden. Remove from fire.
3. Add paneer, parsley, vinegar, cornflour, breadcrumbs, pepper and salt. Mix well. Check salt and pepper.

Spicy Skewers: Recipe on page 22 ➤ *Contd....*

4. Make a small ball of the mixture. Flatten it to give shape of a disc or a kebab. Repeat to make more discs or kebabs.
5. Spread maida in a flat plate. Pat the discs over maida such that it gets coated with maida on all the sides.
6. Heat 2 tbsp oil in a pan and shallow fry 2- 3 discs at a time till well browned. Drain on napkins. Serve hot with poodina chutney.

Note: These discs are very soft from inside. To make them crisp from outside when you add discs to hot oil, shift the earlier ones which are done to the sides of the pan. Let these be there till they turn dark brown and the oil drains out.

Moong Paneer Shooters

Paneer and vegetable sticks, coated with a moong dal batter and fried. The moong dal coating imparts a special flavour to these sticks.

Serves 4

125 gms paneer- cut into ½" thick slices and then into ¾" squares
1 capsicum- cut into 1" pieces
1 tomato - cut into 4 pieces lengthwise, pulp removed and cut into 1" pieces
some chaat masala

BATTER
1 cup dhuli moong dal (dehusked moong beans) - soaked for 1- 2 hours
2 tbsp fresh coriander - chopped very finely, 1 green chilli - chopped very finely
¾ tsp salt, ½ tsp red chilli powder or less, as desired
1- 2 pinches of tandoori red colour

1. Soak dal for 1-2 hours. Strain. Grind in a mixer without water to a smooth thick paste. Put in a bowl. Beat well with hands to make it light.
2. Add coriander, green chilli, salt and chilli powder to the dal paste. Add enough tandoori colour to get a bright orange colour. Keep aside.
3. Sprinkle chat masala nicely on paneer, capsicum & tomato pieces. Mix lightly.
4. Thread a capsicum (wrong side facing you), then a paneer and then a tomato piece (right side facing you) on each tooth pick. Keep aside till serving time.
5. To serve, heat oil for deep frying. Dip the paneer sticks in the prepared dal batter. Coat well with the fingers, sticking the batter nicely.
6. Deep fry till golden. Serve sprinkled with some chaat masala.

Step 4

Curry Patta Toasties : Recipe on page 18, Paneer Mango Submarine: Recipe on page 33

Spicy Skewers

Picture on page 19   Serves 12

150 gms paneer- cut into 1" squares
100 gm baby corns - cut into 2 pieces widthwise
1 large capsicum - cut into ½" pieces
1 tomato - pulp removed and cut into ½" pieces
4-5 flakes garlic - crushed
1 tbsp vinegar
1½ tbsp soya sauce
3 tbsp tomato ketchup
½ tbsp chilli sauce
½ tsp salt and ½ tsp pepper, or to taste
3 tbsp oil

THICK COATING BATTER
¼ cup maida
½ tsp salt, ¼ pepper
¼ cup water

Step 1

1. Cut paneer into 1" squares, capsicum cut into ½" pieces.
2. Cut baby corns widthwise into half to get 2 pieces.
3. Mix all ingredients of the coating batter.
4. Dip the paneer and babycorns in maida batter and deep fry till golden brown. Keep aside.
5. Heat 3 tbsp oil. Reduce heat. Add garlic. Let it turn light brown.

Step 1

6. Remove from fire. Add vinegar, soya sauce, tomato ketchup, chilli sauce, salt and pepper. Return to fire and cook the sauces on low heat for ½ minute.
7. Add baby corns. Stir for 2-3 minutes.
8. Add capsicum, paneer and tomato pieces. Mix well. Stir for 1-2 minutes. Remove from fire.

Step 2

9. Thread a capsicum, then a baby corn, then a paneer and lastly a tomato piece on each tooth pick. Serve.

Step 9

Tandoori

Tips for perfect tandoori cooking (barbecuing)...

- Never over grill paneer. It turns hard on doing so. Also, you can marinate it well in advance but it should be put in a preheated oven just about 20-30 minutes before serving time, so that it can be served straight from the oven. Reheating the paneer can sometimes make it hard. If reheating becomes necessary, brush the tikka nicely with some melted butter before putting it in the oven. Also cover it with some foil so that the direct heat does not affect it and make it hard.

- Tandoori food should be barbecued on the grill rack or wire rack (*jaali*) of the oven and not on the oven tray. When the food is put on the tray, the liquid that drips keeps collecting around the food. This does not let the food get crisp on the outside. When it is on the wire rack, the liquid drips down. These drippings can be collected on a tray covered with aluminium foil and placed under the rack.

- Cut the pieces of paneer according to the space in between the wires of the grill. If the distance between the wires of the rack is too wide, and there is a chance of your piece slipping, then cover the wire rack with a well greased **aluminium foil**.

- The size of tikkas should not be **too small**. After getting cooked they shrink. A very small piece after getting cooked can turn hard.

- While skewering or placing pieces of paneer, the pieces should be arranged such that there is atleast **1" gap** between them so that each piece can get it's own space and heat all around to get cooked properly.

Some Accompaniments to Tandoori Food...

1. Dahi Poodina Chutney:

Hang 1½ cups curd for 15 minutes in a muslin cloth.
Grind ½ cup coriander, ½ cup mint, 2 green chillies, ½ onion and 2 flakes garlic with a little water to a paste. Beat the hung curd well till smooth. Add prepared green paste, 1 tsp oil, pinch of kala namak, ¼ tsp bhuna jeera and salt to taste. Mix, serve.

2. Hot Chilli Garlic Chutney:

4-5 dry red chillies - deseeded and soaked in ¼ cup water, 6 flakes garlic, 1 tsp saboot dhania, 1 tsp jeera, 1 tbsp oil, ½ tsp salt, 1 tsp sugar, 3 tbsp vinegar, ½ tsp soya sauce. For the chutney, grind soaked chillies along with the water, garlic, dhania, jeera, oil and sugar and vinegar to a paste. Add soya sauce. Serve.

Achaari Paneer Tikka

Yellow, pickle flavoured masala paneer tikka.

Picture on page 40   Makes 10-12

400 gms paneer - cut into 1½" rectangles of ¾-1" thickness
2 tsp ginger-garlic paste
1 tsp cornflour
1 cup curd - hang in a muslin cloth for ½ hour
½ tsp haldi (turmeric) powder, 1 tsp amchoor (dried mango powder)
1 tsp dhania powder, ½ tsp garam masala, 1 tsp salt or to taste
½ tsp sugar
1 onion - chopped finely
2 green chillies - chopped
2 tbsp oil, some chaat masala to sprinkle

BASTING (POURING ON THE KEBABS)
some melted butter/oil for basting the tikkas

ACHAARI MASALA
1 tbsp saunf (fennel), ½ tsp sarson (mustard seeds)
a pinch of methi daana (fenugreek seeds)
½ tsp kalonji (onion seeds), ½ tsp jeera (cumin seeds)

1. Collect all the seeds of achaari masala together in a small bowl.
2. Heat oil. Add collected seeds together to the hot oil. Let saunf change colour.
3. Add onions and chopped green chillies. Cook till onions turn golden brown.
4. Reduce heat. Add haldi, amchoor, dhania powder, garam masala, salt and sugar. Mix. Remove from fire. Let it cool down.
5. Beat curd till smooth.
6. Add the onion masala, garlic-ginger paste, and cornflour to the well beaten curd.
7. Add the paneer cubes to the curd. Marinate till serving time.
8. At serving time, rub oil generously over the grill of the oven or wire rack of a gas tandoor. Place paneer on the greased wire rack or grill of the oven.
9. Heat an oven to 180°C or a gas tandoor on moderate flame. Grill paneer for 15 minutes. Spoon some oil or melted butter on the paneer pieces in the oven or tandoor and grill further for 5 minutes. Serve hot sprinkled with chaat masala.

Step 5

Step 6

Haryali Tikka

Serves 6

400 gm paneer - cut into 1½" long pieces, 1" thick
4 tbsp besan (gram flour)
1 tsp salt
4 tbsp oil

GRIND TO A FINE PASTE (CHUTNEY)
1 cup fresh green dhania (green coriander)
2 tsp saunf (fennel)
5-6 flakes garlic
1" piece ginger
4 tbsp lemon juice, ½ tsp salt

1. Cut paneer into 1½" long pieces, 1" thick
2. Grind together dhania, saunf, ginger, garlic, salt and lemon juice to a fine paste.
3. Slit the paneer pieces almost till the end, and keep aside.
4. Divide the chutney into 2 parts.
5. With one part of the chutney, stuff some chutney in the slits of all the paneer pieces. Keep the stuffed paneer aside.
6. Mix together the left over chutney, besan, salt and oil. Rub this all over the stuffed paneer pieces.
7. Rub oil generously over the grill of the oven or wire rack of a gas tandoor. Place paneer on the greased wire rack or grill of the oven.
8. Heat an oven to 180°C or a gas tandoor on moderate flame. Grill paneer for 15 minutes. Spoon some drops of oil on the paneer pieces in the oven or tandoor and grill further for 5-10 minutes. Serve hot.

Note: To cook the tikkas in the oven, place a drip tray under the wire rack on which the tikkas are placed, to collect the drippings.

Step 1

Step 2

Paneer Kakori

Very soft and delicious vegetarian seekh kebabs.

Makes 15

1 cup crumbled or roughly mashed paneer (100 gm)
2 potatoes (medium) - boiled & mashed
2 cups (250 gm) jimikand (yam) - chopped and boiled
½ cup kaju (cashewnuts) - ground
2 tsp ginger- garlic paste
1 onion - very finely chopped
2 green chillies - very finely chopped
2 tbsp green coriander - very finely chopped
1 tsp bhuna jeera (cumin roasted)
1½ tsp salt, 1 tsp red chilli powder
¼ tsp amchoor
3 slices of bread - torn into pieces and churned in a mixer to get fresh crumbs
a pinch of tandoori red colour

INGREDIENTS FOR LATER USE
2 tbsp melted butter or oil, chaat masala

1. Pressure cook chopped yam with ½ cup water and ½ tsp salt to give 3 whistles. Remove from fire. If there is any water in the jimikand, dry it on fire. Mash it with a karchhi or a potato masher on low heat till dry. Remove from fire. Keep aside.
2. Mix paneer, mashed potatoes, jimikand and all other ingredients, making a slightly stiff paste.

   Step 2

3. Rub oil generously on the wire rack or grill of the oven or gas tandoor. Oil and wipe the skewers.
4. Press kebab mixture into finger-shaped kebabs on the skewers. Brush them with oil or rub oil on the palms & shape them with oiled hands. Cook in a tandoor or grill for about 8-10 minutes or till golden brown. Pour some melted butter on the kebabs to baste them. Turn them only when they are almost done otherwise they tend to break. Spoon some oil on the other side also & grill for 5 minutes or till done.
5. Sprinkle tandoori or chaat masala on the kebabs and serve with onion rings sprinkled with lemon juice and chaat masala and lemon wedges.

Note: If you do not wish to grill the kebabs, shallow fry in 1 tbsp oil in a pan, turning sides till browned evenly.

Tikka Reshmi

Tikkas are finished with cream to give them a silky soft taste.

Serves 4-5

250 gms paneer - cut into 1½" cubes (8 pieces)
2 capsicums - cut into 1" pieces
2 onions - cut into 1" pieces
3 tbsp besan (gram flour), 2 tbsp curd
1 tsp salt, ¼ tsp red chilli powder, ½ tsp garam masala
1 tbsp lemon juice, 2 tbsp oil

GRIND TOGETHER TO A PASTE
1½" piece ginger, 3-4 flakes garlic
1 tsp jeera (cumin seeds), seeds of 2 chhoti illaichi
2-3 green chillies, 2 tbsp chopped coriander

OTHER INGREDIENTS
4-5 tbsp thick cream or fresh malai - beaten well till smooth
1 onion - cut into rings
3-4 tbsp chopped poodina (mint) leaves
1 tsp lemon juice, chaat masala

1. Grind garlic, ginger, jeera, chhoti illaichi, coriander and green chillies to a paste.
2. Add besan, curd, salt, chilli powder, garam masala and lemon juice to the paste.
3. Cut paneer into 1½" cubes. Put the paste in a big bowl and add the paneer pieces and mix well so as to coat the paste nicely on all the pieces. Add the onion and capsicum pieces also and mix lightly. Keep aside till serving time.
4. At serving time, rub oil generously over the grill of the oven or wire rack of a gas tandoor. Place paneer on the greased wire rack or grill of the oven.

Step 4

5. Heat an oven to 180°C or a gas tandoor on moderate flame. Grill paneer for 15 minutes. Spoon some oil or melted butter on the paneer pieces in the oven or tandoor and grill further for 5 minutes.
6. Heat malai or cream in a clean kadhai on very low flame, to make it just warm. Do not let it turn into ghee by keeping on the fire for a longer time.
7. Add the grilled paneer and vegetable pieces. Toss gently.
8. Serve on a bed of onion rings sprinkled with some chat masala.

Tandoori Makai Mirch

*Good as a side dish for a meal. Paneer cubes and corn mixed with mozzarella cheese.
On cooking the cheese melts, binding all together.*

Picture on facing page   *Serves 4*

4 medium size capsicums

MARINADE
2 tbsp lemon juice, 1 tsp ginger paste, ½ tsp garlic paste, 1 tbsp oil, ¾ tsp salt

STUFFING
100 gm paneer - finely cut into ¼" cubes (1 cup)
½ cup grated mozzarella cheese
½ cup corn kernels - tinned or freshly boiled
1 tbsp green coriander - chopped
¼ tsp hing (asafoetida)
1 tsp jeera (cumin seeds) and ½ tsp sarson (mustard seeds)
1 small onion - cut into half and then into rings, to get shredded onion
1 tbsp chopped cashews (kaju) and 8-10 raisins (kishmish)
½ tsp red chilli powder, ¾ tsp salt
½ tsp garam masala, ¼ tsp amchoor
BASTING (pouring on the kebabs), 2 tbsp oil or melted butter

1. Cut a thin slice from the top (stem end) of each capsicum. Scoop out the center with the help of a knife. Mix all the ingredients of the marinade and rub liberally on the inside of the capsicums. Cover with caps and leave aside for ½ hour.

2. Take a heavy bottom kadhai and heat 2 tbsp oil. Put in the hing, jeera, and sarson. Wait till jeera turns golden.

3. Add onions and cook till golden brown. Add cashews and kishmish. Stir. Add red chilli powder, salt, garam masala and amchoor.

4. Add corn and cook for 1 minute. Add paneer and mix well. Remove from fire. Add mozzarella cheese. Mix. Keep filling aside.

5. Stuff the capsicums with this filling. They should be stuffed well but not to bursting point. Rub oil on the outside of the stuffed capsicums. Cover with the caps and secure them with wooden tooth-picks.

6. Oil and wipe the skewers. Skewer the capsicums. Small onions or pieces of potatoes can be used in-between to prevent them from slipping. Put the skewers into the gas tandoor or oven and cook for 10 minutes or till they turn blackish at some places. Turn 1-2 times in-between to grill evenly. Serve.

Note: Capsicums can be placed on the wire-rack or grill rubbed with some oil, if you don't have skewers. It is then not necessary to fasten them with tooth picks.

Paneer Tikka

Serves 4

300 gm paneer - cut into 1½" squares of 1" thickness
1 large capsicum - deseeded and cut into 1" pieces (12 pieces)
1 onion - cut into 4 pieces and then separated

MARINADE
½ cup dahi- hang in a muslin cloth for 15 minutes
3 tbsp thick malai or thick cream
a few drops of orange colour or a pinch of haldi (turmeric)
1½ tbsp oil, 1 tbsp (level) cornflour
½ tsp amchoor, ½ tsp kala namak, ¾ tsp salt, or to taste
1 tbsp tandoori masala

GRIND TOGETHER
1" piece ginger, 5-6 flakes garlic
2 dried, whole red chillies - soaked in water for 10 minutes and drained

Step 1

1. Hang curd in a muslin cloth for 15 minutes.
2. Drain soaked red chillies. Grind ginger, garlic and red chillies to a paste.
3. To the ginger-garlic-chilli paste, add hung dahi, cream or malai, 1½ tbsp oil, 1 tbsp cornflour, amchoor, salt, kala namak, tandoori masala, colour or haldi and paneer. Mix well.
4. Brush the wire rack (grill) of the oven generously with oil.
5. Arrange paneer on a greased wire rack of the oven or on the skewers. After all the paneer pieces are done, put the capsicum and onions - both together in the left over marinade and mix well to coat the vegetables with the marinade. Leave the vegetables in the bowl itself.

Step 3

6. At the time of serving, put the paneer pieces placed on the wire rack in the hot oven at about 200°C. Grill till almost done, for about 15 minutes. Grill the paneer till it gets dry and starts getting crisp. Sprinkle some oil on the paneer pieces. Now remove the vegetables from the bowl and put them also in the oven on the sides of the paneer. Grill everything together for another 5 minutes. The vegetables should not be grilled for too long.
7. Remove from the oven. Serve immediately (really hot), sprinkled with some lemon juice and chaat masala.

◄ *Broccoli Bonanza: Recipe on page 65*

Naaza

Teatime &
Snacky Meals

Quiche

Pasta

Paneer Mango Submarine

These are not served hot like the usual footlongs. An Ideal low calorie snack for summers.

Serves 6   *Picture on page 20*

1 long French bread or garlic bread - cut lengthwise to get 2 thin, long pieces
2 tbsp butter - softened, 2 tbsp oil
2 tbsp sweet mango chutney (home made or fun food)
1 kheera - cut into round slices without peeling
2 firm tomatoes - cut into slices
few poodina (mint) leaves to garnish - dipped in chilled water

SPRINKLE ON PANEER
400 gm paneer - cut into ¼" thick round slices with a kulfi mould cover
¼ tsp haldi
½ tsp chilli powder, ½ tsp salt
1 tsp chaat masala powder

1. Spread butter on the cut surface of both the pieces of bread, as well as a little on the sides. Place the breads in the oven at 200°C on a wire rack for 10-12 minutes till crisp and light brown on the cut surface. Keep aside.

2. Cut paneer into ¼" thick slices and then cut the slices into round pieces with a kulfi mould (saancha) cover or a biscuit cutter or a sharp lid of any bottle.

Step 2

3. Sprinkle paneer on both sides with some chilli powder, salt, haldi and chaat masala.

4. At serving time, heat 2 tbsp oil in a non stick pan. Saute paneer pieces on both sides in 2 tbsp oil till slightly toasted to a nice yellowish-brown colour.

Step 7

5. To assemble the submarine, apply 1 tbsp mango chutney on each piece of bread.

6. Sprinkle some chaat masala on the kheera and tomato pieces. Sprinkle some chat masala on the paneer also.

7. Place a piece of paneer, then kheera, then tomato and keep repeating all three in the same sequence so as to cover the loaf. Keep paneer, kheera and tomato, slightly overlapping. Insert fresh mint leaves in between the vegetables, so that they show. Serve.

Note: Mango chutney is available in bottles in stores.

Chargrilled Caprika Pizza

This quick home made pizza of an unusual shape has a smoky flavour of roasted coloured capsicums. Do not wash the capsicums after roasting or you will lose flavour, so wash before you roast them.

Makes 3

THIN CRUSTY HOME MADE PIZZA BASE
¼ cup lukewarm water
½ tsp sugar
2 tsp heaped dried yeast (10 gms)
1 teacup milk
1½ tbsp oil
1 tsp salt
1 tsp sugar
300 gms (3 packed cups) maida (plain flour)

TOPPING
1 large green capsicum - cut into half and deseeded
1 large red capsicum - cut into half and deseeded
1 large yellow capsicum - cut into half and deseeded
2- 3 big mushrooms, optional
1 onion - cut into half and sliced to get semi circles
salt and oregano or pepper to taste
1 tbsp oil
2 tbsp fresh parsley leaves - chopped finely or 1 tsp dry parsley
100 gms paneer - grated finely (1 cup)
150 gm grated mozzarella cheese (1½ cups)
3 tbsp melted butter or olive oil

1. Mix warm water and sugar in a cup. Feel the water with a finger to check if it is lukewarm. Add yeast. Shake the cup gently to mix the yeast. Cover the cup and leave it in a warm place till the granules of the yeast disappear and it becomes frothy. (10-15 minutes). (If it does not swell, discard it).

2. Mix milk, oil, salt and sugar in a pan. Keep aside. When the yeast becomes frothy, heat this milk mixture to make it lukewarm. Add the ready yeast mix to the luke warm milk mixture. Add this yeast and milk mixture to the maida and knead well to make a smooth dough.

3. Grease a big polythene bag, brush the dough with a little oil and put it in the polythene. Keep it covered in a warm place to swell for 1 hour or till it is double in size.

Contd...

4. Now punch it down to its original size, brush with oil and keep it back in the polythene bag for another 15 minutes or till it swells again.

5. Make 3 balls. Spread a 10" square aluminium foil on a kitchen platform. Grease it with some oil. Flatten a ball of the dough on it using the fingers to a thin rectangular-oval pizza of about 10"x7" size. Prick each base with a fork. Brush pizza base with olive oil or any oil. Keep aside.

6. Wash and rub oil on the skin of the capsicums and mushrooms. Insert a fork or a knife on to the greased capsicums and mushrooms. Roast on a naked flame, turning sides, directly on the heat till charred (slightly blackened) from various sides. Roast for 2-3 minutes. Cool. Cut the smoked capsicum into 1" pieces and cut the mushroom each lengthwise into 3-4 thick slices. OR, Put them under the grill, skin side up till the skin is evenly charred with black spots. Remove from grill. Leave covered for 5-10 minutes. Do not wash even if there are some black patches left. (They taste and look good!). Chop into 1" pieces.

Step 6

7. Sprinkle some grated cheese and paneer over the base. Sprinkle parsley. Arrange roasted capsicums, mushrooms and onion. Sprinkle salt and oregano. Top with more grated cheese.

8. Drizzle some olive oil. Place the pizza with the aluminium foil on the wire rack of the oven (not tray) and bake at 180°C (350°F) for 15 minutes until golden and crisp.

Cheesy Broccoli Wraps

Quick wraps which can be enjoyed as a complete roll for dinner or cut into pieces for tea.

Serves 4

DOUGH

¾ cup maida (plain flour), 1 tbsp oil, ½ tsp salt, a pinch of baking powder

FILLING FOR 4 WRAPS

**1 small broccoli- cut the thick stem and peel and slice stem, cut head into florets
with thin stems, 1 onion - cut into rings
100 gms paneer- cut into tiny squares
1 tsp jeera (cumin seeds), 1 tsp finely chopped garlic
½ tsp dhania powder, ½ tsp garam masala, ¼ tsp amchoor, ¼ tsp haldi
1 tomato - chopped, 1 tsp salt, or to taste, 1 tbsp lemon juice
3- 4 tbsp readymade mayonnaise or mustard sauce, 2 tbsp tomato ketchup**

1. Make a firm dough of flour, oil, baking powder and salt, using water. Keep covered for 20 minutes.
2. Heat 3 tbsp oil for filling. Add jeera and garlic. Wait till it changes colour. Add onion rings and stir till soft.
3. Add broccoli florets and stem. Stir fry for 2-3 minutes. Add dhania powder, garam masala, amchoor and haldi. Add paneer and tomato, stir for 1-2 minutes.
4. Add lemon juice and salt to taste. Remove from fire.
5. Make 4 small balls of the dough. Roll them into thin chappatis with the maida dough, cooking them very lightly on both sides on a tawa (griddle) on low heat.
6. Spread some mayonnaise or mustard on each chappati nicely all over.
7. Spread some vegetable mixture on the roti. (See picture given below). Roll up the roti tightly. Seal the ends with some tomato ketchup. Keep aside with the joint side down, so that the wraps get well sealed.
8. To serve, heat 1 tbsp oil and panfry the wrap first with the tucked side down till golden. Turn and fry till golden on both sides.

Step 3

Add broccoli and stir fry for few minutes.

Step 7

Moong Dal Chillahs with Paneer

Serves 4

1 cup moong dal (split green gram)
½ tsp salt
½ tsp red chilli powder
1½ tbsp finely chopped coriander
150-200 gms paneer (cottage cheese) - cut into 3" long fingers
2 tbsp oil
½ tsp salt, ½ tsp garam masala
½ tsp red chilli powder
1 tbsp chopped coriander

1. Soak dal for 3-4 hours only. Do not soak for a longer period.
2. Strain. Grind with 1 cup water to a smooth batter. Add about ½ cup water to get a pouring consistency.
3. Add ½ tsp salt, ½ tsp chilli powder and coriander. Keep aside.
4. Prepare the paneer by heating 2 tbsp oil in a non-stick pan. Add ½ tsp salt, ½ tsp garam masala and ½ tsp red chilli powder. Shut off the gas.
5. Add paneer pieces and coriander. Mix gently with the oil.
6. Return to fire, fry for a few seconds. Remove from pan. Keep aside.
7. Heat a non-stick pan (not too hot), smear 1 tsp oil in the centre.
8. Spread one karchhi (¼ cup) of batter to make a chillah of about 4" diameter.

9. Pour some oil on the sides.
10. Turn over.
11. Heat one prepared paneer piece on the side of the pan.
12. Remove chillah and paneer from the pan.
13. Place the paneer piece at one end of the chillah. Roll it up.
14. Serve hot with poodina chutney or any other sauce.
15. To make the next chillah, put off the gas. Cool the pan by sprinkling some water. Wipe clean.
16. Smear 1 tsp oil in the centre. Spread a karchhi of batter.
17. Return to fire and proceed as before. Serve hot.

Toasted Sandwiches

Toasted bread sandwiched with sauted slices of potatoes, paneer and cabbage leaves.

Makes 8 sandwiches

8 cabbage leaves (take 1 small cabbage) - each torn into 2 pieces
3-4 firm tomatoes - cut into slices
2 big boiled potatoes - sliced
250 gms paneer
salt and pepper to taste
cheese spread - enough to spread
3-4 tbsp butter
8 bread slices

1. Cut paneer and potatoes into thin slices.
2. Heat 2 tbsp butter in a nonstick pan. Put a slice of potato on it and then shift to the side. Turn when the under side is light brown. Put more slices in the centre and brown them.
3. Repeat with all other potato slices. Let them be on the sides of the pan.
4. Put some more butter. Saute the paneer slightly. Shift to the sides.
5. Place the cabbage leaves also on the hot pan. Remove from heat. Leave everything in the pan.
6. Lightly toast the bread slices. Spread cheese spread on one side and some butter on the other side of all slices.
7. On each toast spread some cabbage leaves on the cheese spread.
8. Cover the leaves with 2-3 potato slices. Sprinkle salt and pepper. Put paneer slices over the potatoes. Put tomato slices over the paneer.
9. Cover with another toasted slice, keeping the buttered side on the outside. Press gently. Keep aside till serving time.
10. To serve, heat on the pan till the bread turns crisp. Cut into 2 halves and serve with tomato ketchup or mustard sauce.

Step 2 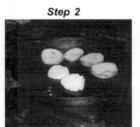   *Step 4* 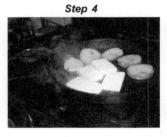   *Step 8*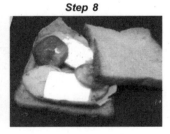

Deep Dish Quiche: Recipe on page 46 ➢

Cheesy Tomato Pasta

Serves 2

1½ cups unboiled pasta (penne or any other pasta) - boiled (about 3 cups)
½ cup (50 gm) - roughly mashed paneer
½ cup grated cheddar cheese (Britannia cubes)- grated
¼ cup milk, approx.
1 small flower of broccoli (150 gms)
3 tbsp olive oil or butter
2 onions - finely chopped
4- 5 flakes of garlic- crushed
250 gm tomatoes - blanched in hot water, skinned and chopped finely
1 tomato - pureed in a mixer
8-10 basil leaves or tender tulsi leaves
1½ tsp salt, ½ tsp pepper
1 tsp oregano or ¾ tsp ajwain (carom seeds)

Step 1

1. Cut broccoli into very small florets with very little stalk, (about 2 cups chopped).
2. For boiling pasta, boil 8 cups of water with 2 tsp salt. When the water starts to boil, add pasta to the pan. Stir well. Boil for about 4-5 minutes till almost done. Remove from fire and leave it in hot water for 2-3 minutes. Strain.
3. Add fresh water to refresh the pasta and strain again. Sprinkle 1 tbsp olive oil on the pasta. Keep aside.

Step 4

4. To blanch tomatoes, put tomatoes in a pan with some water. Boil for 2-3 minutes. Remove from water and peel the skin of tomatoes and chop finely.
5. Heat 3 tbsp oil or butter. Add onion and garlic, cook until onions turn soft.
6. Add tomatoes, fresh tomato puree, basil leaves, salt, pepper and oregano. Cook for 2 minutes, stirring occasionally.
7. Add broccoli, mix well for 1-2 minutes till crisp-tender. Do not over cook. Keep sauce aside. Let the broccoli be crisp and crunchy.
8. At the time of serving, heat sauce, add pasta, paneer, cheese and milk. Mix well. Remove from fire. Transfer to a serving platter. Serve hot with garlic bread.

◄ *Achaari Paneer Tikka: Recipe on page 24*

Chilli Paneer Dosa

Regular dosa with a different filling. Give it a try, you will forget the potato filling!

Picture on page 49   *Makes 10*

DOSA
½ cup sela or ushna chaawal (boiled rice) of ordinary quality
1¼ cups permal chaawal (ordinary quality rice)
½ cup dhuli urad dal (dehusked black gram dal)
1 tsp methi dana (fenugreek seeds)
1 tsp salt

TOMATO SPREAD
15 flakes garlic - crushed
¾ tsp red chilli paste or powder
1½ cups ready made tomato puree
6 tbsp tomato ketchup
1½ tsp oregano (dried) or ¾ tsp ajwain (carom seeds)
salt and pepper to taste
2 tbsp oil

CHILLI PANEER
300 gms paneer - cut into ½" cubes
1½ capsicums - chopped
1½ tbsp soya sauce, 1½ tbsp vinegar
¾ tsp salt, ¾ tsp pepper
1½ tsp red chilli paste or red chilli powder
1½ tsp garlic paste (8 garlic flakes - crushed)

1. Soak both rice, dal and fenugreek seeds together in a pan for atleast 6 hours.
2. Grind together finely to a paste, using some of the water in which it was soaked.
3. Add more water to the paste, if required, to get a paste of medium pouring consistency. Add salt. Mix well.
4. Keep aside for 12 hours or overnight in a warm place, to get fermented. After fermentation, the batter should rise a little and smell sour.
5. Mix paneer with soya sauce, vinegar, salt, pepper, chilli paste and crushed garlic. Keep aside to marinate for 15 minutes.
6. Sprinkle some maida on the paneer. Mix gently to coat. Deep fry till golden.

Step 6

7. Crush the fried paneer with fingers into crumbs. Add capsicum and ½ tsp soya sauce. Check salt.

8. To prepare the spread, heat 2 tbsp oil. Add garlic and cook till light brown. Add all the other ingredients and cook on low flame till it turns to a thick paste.

9. For dosas, mix the batter nicely with a karchhi, before preparing dosas.

10. Heat a non stick tawa on medium flame. Pour a tsp oil on the tawa. Sprinkle a pinch of salt on the oil. Rub the tawa with piece of old cloth or paper napkin.

11. Remove tawa from fire and pour 1 heaped karchhi of batter. Spread quickly.

12. Return to fire. Cook till the dosa gets little cooked.

13. Pour 2 tsp of oil upon the dosa and the sides. Cover for 1-2 minutes.

Step 15, 16

14. After it turns golden brown, gently loosen the sides and bottom.

15. Drop small dots of tomato spread, in different places on the dosa and spread quickly with the back of a spoon, covering the edges completely.

16. Put 3 tbsp of the filling in the centre of the dosa in a row and spread a little.

17. Fold over from both sides. Remove from tawa. Cut it from the middle diagonally to get 2 small pieces. Serve hot with coconut chutney.

Tip: For a party you can cut each dosa into four pieces diagonally like you do for a spring roll.

Mexican Fajita

Fa-hi-taa, (the alphabet 'j' is pronounced as 'h'). There is no hard and fast rule for making the roll of fajita. You can serve all the things together in a platter to the guests & ask them to make their own roll or wrap!

Makes 5-6

7 FLOUR TORTILLAS
1½ cups maida (plain flour)
1 tsp baking powder, ½ tsp salt
warm water to knead

VEGETABLE FILLING
150 gms paneer - cut into ¼" thick, long pieces
¼ of a small cauliflower - cut into small florets
½ of a small cabbage- shredded
½ cup French beans - sliced diagonally
2-3 carrots - sliced diagonally
2 dry, red chillies - crushed
1 tsp vinegar, ½ tsp salt, ½ tsp freshly ground peppercorns
3 tbsp olive oil or any cooking oil, 1 tbsp butter
1 onion- sliced, 6 flakes garlic - crushed
2 tbsp chopped coriander
2 tsp white wine (optional)

SALAD
3-4 lettuce leaves - shredded
1- 2 spring onions - chopped till the greens, ½ tsp salt
1 tomato - chopped, 1 green chilli - chopped
½ cup cheddar cheese - grated (50 gms)

SOUR CREAM
¾ cup thick curd - hang for ½ hour in a cloth and whip till smooth
½ cup cream - whip till thick, few drops Tabasco sauce, salt to taste

SALSA
5 tomatoes - roasted, 1 tbsp oil
2 onions - chopped finely
2 green chillies - chopped, 2 tbsp chopped coriander
1 tbsp tomato ketchup, 1 tsp vinegar, ½ tsp salt and ¼ tsp pepper, or to taste

1. Sift maida with baking powder and salt. Add warm water very gradually and bind together roughly. Knead with wet hands till a smooth and elastic dough is ready.
2. Make 7 equal balls. Cover with a plastic wrap or a cling film or a damp cloth and keep aside for 15 minutes.

Contd...

3. Roll out each ball into a tortilla, using a little maida till you get a very thin round of about 8-9" diameter.
4. Heat a tawa (griddle). Cook lightly on one side for about a minute and then turn. Reduce heat and cook the other side also for a minute till light brown specs appear. Wrap in an aluminium foil and keep aside in a casserole. Make all tortillas similarly.
5. For the filling, mix paneer, cauliflower, cabbage, beans, carrots, red chilli, salt, pepper, 1 tbsp oil and vinegar. Keep aside for half an hour in the refrigerator.
6. For salad, mix all ingredients of the salad in a bowl. Mix well.
7. For sour cream, beat hung curd, salt, tabasco sauce and cream till smooth. Keep aside.
8. For salsa, pierce a tomato with a fork. Hold it over the naked flame to roast it till the skin turns blackish and charred. Roast all the tomatoes like this. Cool the tomatoes and peel. Chop 2 tomatoes and puree the other 3 tomatoes.
    Heat oil and saute onion and green chillies till onion turns soft. Add all other ingredients and cook for 2-3 minutes. Remove from fire.
9. To prepare the filling, heat 2 tbsp oil and 1 tbsp butter. Cook onions and garlic till soft. Except paneer add all the marinated vegetables. Stir- fry for 5-7 minutes on moderate heat till tender but still remain crisp. Add coriander, wine, paneer, ¾ tsp salt and ½ tsp pepper or to taste. Cook for 2-3 minutes. Remove from fire.
10. To serve, put sour cream, salad and salsa in separate bowls. Serve tortillas wrapped in a napkin in a casserole or basket.
11. Serve the vegetable filling separately in a sizzler plate.
12. Make your own roll. Take one tortilla, spread 1-2 tsp of the sour cream on the whole tortilla spreading till the sides, then spread some vegetables on it, then sprinkle some salad and finally pour 1½ tbsp salsa. Roll and enjoy.

Step 11

Vegetable filling of fajitas served in a sizzler plate

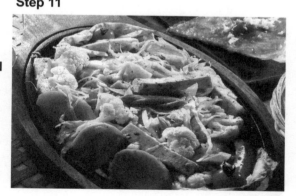

Deep Dish Quiche

Picture on page 39   Serves 6

SHELL
¼ cup melted butter
1¼ cups plain flour (maida), a pinch of baking powder
¼ cup grated cheese, 3 tbsp water, or as required

VEGETABLES FOR FILLING
1 cup baked beans (tinned) or corn kernels (freshly boiled or tinned)
2 cups sliced mushrooms, ½ cup grated paneer, 1 onion - finely chopped
½ tsp salt and ¼ tsp pepper, 1 tbsp butter - softened

MIX TOGETHER
6 tbsp cream, 2 tbsp tomato puree, 1½ tbsp cornflour
½ tsp salt, ¼ tsp freshly ground pepper, 2 tbsp chopped fresh parsley or coriander

OTHER INGREDIENTS
1½ cups (150 gm) grated mozzarella or pizza cheese
½ tsp dried oregano, a few tomato slices

1. Sift flour and baking powder. Combine butter with flour, rubbing well until it looks like bread crumbs. Add cheese. Add just enough water to bind & knead lightly to a firm dough. Chill the dough, well covered in a wet muslin cloth for 30 minutes.
2. Roll out to a thin chappati, slightly bigger than the baking flan tin (a shallow tin with a loose bottom.) Roll out and place it in the baking flan tin. Press the mixture well to cover the base and the sides too. Press carefully to get a well levelled base. Trim the excess by rolling a rolling pin on the edges of the tin.
3. Prick with a fork all over to avoid the crust from puffing up during baking.
4. Bake the quiche crusts in a hot oven (200°C/390°F), for about 10-15 minutes, until light golden yellow. Allow to cool.
5. To prepare the filling, heat butter. Add onions. Cook till soft. Add mushrooms and cook until water evaporates and they turn dry. Add corn or beans & paneer. Add ½ tsp salt and ¼ tsp pepper. Cook for a few seconds. Remove from fire.
6. In a cup, mix together – cream, tomato puree, cornflour, salt, pepper & parsley.
7. Spoon the mushroom-paneer mix into a cooled quiche crust and level it.
8. Sprinkle ¼ cup grated cheese on it, keeping some for the top.
9. Spread the cream-tomato puree mixture on the cheese. Sprinkle with the remaining cheese.
10. Sprinkle some oregano. Arrange a few halved slices of tomato.
11. Bake in a preheated oven set at 190°C/375°F for about 25 minutes or until the filling is set and the top is golden. Allow to cool before serving.

Naaza

A great combination of Pizza & Naan! Naan spread with an Indian tomato spread flavoured with kasoori methi, topped with paneer tikkas & mozzarella cheese & grilled in the oven.

Serves 4   *Picture on page 32*

2 ready made nans
100-150 gms pizza cheese

TOMATO SPREAD
1-2 tbsp oil, 4 flakes garlic - crushed
2 small tomatoes - pureed in a mixer
¼ tsp salt, ¼ tsp garam masala, ¼ tsp red chilli powder
2 tbsp tomato sauce
2 tsp kasoori methi (dry fenugreek leaves)

PANEER TOPPING
100 gms paneer - cut into ½" squares
2 tsp kasoori methi (dry fenugreek leaves)
½ green and ½ yellow capsicum - cut into ½" squares, or 1 green one
1 tomato - cut into 4 pieces, deseeded and cut into ½" pieces
½ onion - cut into ½" squares
¼ tsp each - salt, red chilli powder, haldi and garam masala, or to taste
1 tbsp tomato puree
½ tsp ginger-garlic paste

YOGURT CHUTNEY (MIX EVERYTHING TOGETHER)
2 tbsp hari chutney, 3 tbsp curd - whipped till smooth
a pinch of kala namak and bhuna jeera, 1 tsp oil or cream

1. For the tomato spread, heat oil. Add garlic and all other ingredients. Cook till thick.
2. For the paneer topping, heat 1½ tbsp oil. Add onion. Saute till golden. Reduce heat. Add salt, red chilli powder, haldi and garam masala. Mix. Add tomato puree and ginger- garlic paste. Add capsicums and tomato. Mix.
3. Add paneer and kasoori methi. Mix well and remove from fire.
4. Brush naan with 1 tsp oil. Spread some tomato spread, covering well till edges.
5. Sprinkle some pizza cheese. Spread paneer topping. Sprinkle some cheese again.
6. Grill for about 15 minutes at 200°C till the paneer gets grilled and the edges of the naan turn brown. Do not over grill, it turns hard!
7. Cut into rectangular pieces and serve hot with yogurt chutney.

Indian Meal Time Dishes
Dry & Masala

Chilli Paneer Dosa: Recipe on page 42 ➢

Hari Chutney Paneer

Chatpata paneer dish which goes very well as a side dish.

Serves 4   *Picture on opposite page*

200 gms paneer - cut into about 1" big triangular pieces of ¼" thickness
1½ cups of curd - hang in a muslin cloth for 20 minutes
4 flakes garlic and ½" piece of ginger - crush to a paste or 1 tsp ginger-garlic paste
¼ tsp jeera (cumin seeds), 3 tbsp oil
1 onion - sliced thinly
¾ tsp chaat masala - to sprinkle on paneer

CHUTNEY (GRIND TOGETHER)
½ cup poodina (mint)
½ cup hara dhania (green coriander)
2 green chillies, 1 onion
½ tsp kala namak (black salt), ½ tsp bhuna jeera (roasted cumin)
½ tsp salt or to taste, ¼ tsp powdered sugar

1. Hang curd in a muslin cloth for 20 minutes.
2. For chutney, wash coriander and mint leaves.
3. Grind together all the ingredients given under chutney to a paste. Keep the chutney aside.
4. Beat hung curd well till smooth.
5. To the hung curd, add the chutney. Keep aside.
6. Cut the block of paneer into rectangular slices of about ¼" thickness. Now cut each slice into 2 triangular pieces. Do not make the pieces too thick.
7. Cut each piece further into 2 triangles if the piece is big. Sprinkle chaat masala on the paneer. Mix gently.
8. Heat oil in a kadhai, add jeera and ginger-garlic paste. Cook for few seconds.
9. Add sliced onion and cook till golden.
10. Reduce heat and add the dahi-chutney. Cook for 2-3 minutes on low heat, stirring in between. Check salt. Keep aside.
11. At the time of serving, add paneer pieces to the chutney and mix gently but thoroughly to coat the pieces nicely with chutney. Heat on low fire. Serve.

Step 4

Step 6

Step 11
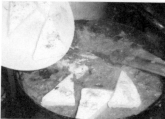

◁ *Jalapeno & Cheese Croquettes: Recipe on page 11, Hari Chutney Paneer*

Paneer in Imli Chutney

Paneer & peanuts in tamarind flavoured masala. Try it as a filling for dosas too. You'll Love it.

Serves 4-6

**250 gms of paneer- cut into 1" square pieces
4 tbsp oil, 2 onions - sliced
2 tbsp roasted peanuts (moongphali), 1½ tsp ginger- garlic paste
2 tbsp chopped coriander**

**ROAST TOGETHER ON TAWA TILL FRAGRANT
3-4 laung (cloves), 1" stick dalchini (cinnamon)
seeds of 2 moti illaichi (black cardamom)
3 saboot kali mirch (pepper corns)**

**SPICED IMLI CHUTNEY
a lemon sized ball of imli (tamarind)
½ tsp kala namak (rock salt), ¼ tsp salt, 1 tsp dhania (coriander) powder
½ tsp red chilli powder, ½ tsp garam masala, 1¼ tsp sugar**

Step 1

1. Soak imli in ½ cup water for ½ hour. Give one boil.
2. Sieve through a strainer. Strain well to get thick imli water. Reserve the imli water. Discard the residue in the strainer.
3. Roast laung, dalchini, moti illaichi and saboot kali mirch on a tawa. Crush together to a rough powder on a chakla belan.

Step 2

4. Mix roasted spices, kala namak, salt, dhania powder, red chilli powder, garam masala and sugar to the imli water. Cook it on low flame in a pan till it reaches a sauce like consistency. Keep imli chutney aside.
5. Heat 4 tbsp oil in a kadhai. Add sliced onion and cook till light brown.
6. Add peanuts and ginger-garlic paste. Saute for 2 minutes.

Step 6

7. Add imli chutney, cook for 2 minutes on low heat.
8. Add ½ cup water. Give one boil. Remove from fire.
9. Add coriander and paneer pieces (see note). Mix well.
10. At serving time, heat thoroughly and serve hot.

Note: You can also deep fry the paneer pieces till golden, before adding to the masala.

Achaari Paneer

Pickled flavoured masala paneer.

Serves 8

300 gms paneer - cut into 1½" cubes
2 capsicums - cut into 2" pieces
1" piece ginger & 5-6 flakes garlic - crushed to a paste
1 cup curd - beat well till smooth
3 onions - chopped finely
4 green chillies - chopped
½ tsp haldi (turmeric) powder, ¾ tsp garam masala
1 tsp amchoor (dried mango powder) or lemon juice to taste
2-3 green chillies - cut lengthwise into 4 pieces
1 tsp salt or to taste
½ cup milk
¼ cup cream

ACHAARI MASALA
2 tsp saunf (aniseeds), 1 tsp rai (mustard seeds)
a pinch of methi daana (fenugreek seeds)
½ tsp kalonji (onion seeds), 1 tsp jeera (cumin seeds)

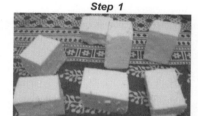

Step 1

1. Cut paneer into 1½" cubes.
2. Sprinkle ½ tsp haldi, a pinch of salt and ½ tsp red chilli powder on the paneer and capsicum. Mix well. Keep aside for 10 minutes.
3. Collect all seeds of the achaari masala - saunf, rai, methi dana, kalonji and jeera together.
4. Crush garlic and ginger roughly or use 2 tsp ginger-garlic paste.
5. Heat 4 tbsp oil. Add the collected seeds together to the hot oil. Let them crackle for 1 minute or till jeera turns golden.
6. Add onions and chopped green chillies. Cook till onions turn golden.
7. Add haldi and garlic-ginger paste. Cook for ½ minute.
8. Reduce heat. Beat curd with 2 tbsp water and a pinch of haldi till smooth. Add gradually and keep stirring. Add amchoor, garam masala and ¾ tsp salt or to taste. Cook for 2-3 minutes on low heat till the curd dries up a little. (Do not make it very dry). Remove from fire and let it cool down.
9. At the time of serving, add milk and slit green chillies. Boil on low heat for a minute, stirring continuously. Cook on low flame for 2-3 minutes.
10. Add cream, paneer and capsicum, cook for 1-2 minutes on low flame. Serve.

Paneer Jalfrezi

Paneer deliciously combined with mixed vegetables.

Picture on page 88   Serves 4

150 gm paneer - cut into thin long pieces
8-10 french beans - sliced diagonally into 1" pieces
1 large carrot - cut diagonally into thin slices
½ green capsicum - deseed and cut into thin fingers
½ yellow or red pepper (capsicum) - deseeded & sliced into thin fingers
½ cup boiled peas (matar)
1 long, firm tomato - cut into 4, pulp removed and cut into thin long pieces
15-20 curry leaves, 3 tbsp oil

COLLECT TOGETHER IN A PLATE
½ tsp jeera (cumin seeds)
¼ tsp sarson (mustard seeds), ¼ tsp kalonji (onion seeds)
¼ tsp methi daana (fenugreek seeds)

MIX TOGETHER
½ cup tomato puree
1 tsp tomato ketchup
2 tsp ginger-garlic paste or 2 tsp ginger-garlic - finely chopped
½ tsp red chilli powder, 1 tsp dhania powder
½ tsp amchoor powder, 1 tsp salt

1. Mix together - tomato puree, tomato ketchup, ginger-garlic, red chilli powder, dhania powder, amchoor and salt in a cup. Keep aside.
2. Heat 3 tbsp oil in a kadhai. Add the collected seeds together. When jeera turns golden, reduce heat and add curry leaves and stir for a few seconds.
3. Add the tomato puree mixed with dry masalas and stir on medium heat for 2 minutes.
4. Add carrot and beans. Stir for 1 minute.
5. Add ¼ cup water. Cover the kadhai. Cook on low heat for about 4-5 minutes, till vegetables are cooked but still remain crunchy.
6. Add the capsicums, boiled peas, paneer and tomato slices. Stir till well blended. Remove from fire. Serve hot.

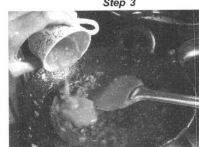

Step 3

Paneer Dil Bahaar

A quick way of preparing a different paneer dish. A little besan (gramflour) makes all the difference.

Serves 6

250 gms paneer - cut into 1½" cubes
2 capsicums - cut into 1" pieces
2 small onions - cut into 1" pieces
½ tsp garam masala, ½ tsp red chilli powder, ½ tsp salt
2 tsp kasoori methi (dried fenugreek leaves)
2-3 tsp besan (gram flour), juice of ½ lemon

PASTE
1" piece of ginger, 3-4 flakes garlic
2 dry, red chillies
2 green chillies

OTHER INGREDIENTS TO BE ADDED TO THE PASTE
¼ tsp haldi (turmeric powder), ½ tsp ajwain (carom seeds)
2 tbsp malai or thick cream
1 tsp oil, ½ tsp salt

1. Cut paneer into 1½ cubes, capsicum and onion into 1" pieces.
2. Grind all the ingredients given under paste to a rough paste- ginger, garlic, green and red chillies.
2. Add haldi, ajwain, malai or cream, oil and salt to the ginger-garlic-chilli paste.
3. Rub this paste all over on paneer pieces. Keep aside for 10 minutes.
4. Heat 2 tbsp oil. Add capsicum and onion pieces. Cook for 2 minutes on low flame. Add ½ tsp garam masala, ½ tsp red chilli powder and ½ tsp salt.
5. Add paneer pieces.
6. Add kasoori methi. Mix. Sprinkle 2-3 tsp besan. Cook on low flame, stirring continuously till paneer gets coated a little with besan.
7. Sprinkle some red chilli powder and lemon juice. Stir fry for 2 minutes on low flame. Serve hot.

Step 1   Step 1   Step 1

Makhmali Paneer Masala

Paneer pieces coated with curd and gramflour and fried to make them as soft as velvet.

Serves 3-4

250 gms paneer - cut into 1½" cubes
3 tbsp besan (gram flour)
2 tbsp curd
1 tsp salt, ¼ tsp red chilli powder
a few drops orange red colour
2 capsicums - cut into 1" pieces
2 onions - cut into 1" pieces
1 tbsp tomato puree, ½ tsp garam masala
2 tbsp oil

PASTE
1½" piece ginger, 3-4 flakes garlic
1 tsp jeera (cumin seeds)
seeds of 2 chhoti illaichi (green cardamoms)
2-3 green chillies
2 tbsp chopped coriander
1 tbsp lemon juice

1. Grind together all the ingredients given under paste to a smooth paste.
2. Add besan, curd, salt and chilli powder to the paste. Add enough orange colour to the paste to get a nice colour.
3. Cut paneer into 1½" cubes. Put the paste in a big bowl and add the paneer pieces and mix well so as to coat the paste nicely on all the pieces. Add the onion and capsicum pieces also and mix lightly. Keep aside till serving time.

   Step 4

4. Heat oil for frying. Pick up only the paneer pieces, leaving the vegetables and deep fry few paneer pieces at a time till slightly crisp. Keep aside till serving time. Let the onion and capsicum be in the masala in the bowl and keep in the fridge.
5. At the time of serving, heat 2 tbsp oil in a kadhai. Add onion and capsicum pieces. Stir for a few minutes till onions turn soft. Add ¼ tsp salt.
6. Add tomato puree and cook for a minute on low heat.
7. Add fried paneer pieces. Sprinkle garam masala. Toss for a minute till the paneer turns hot and soft. Serve immediately.

Paneer Spring Onion

Paneer with green onions.

Serves 4

200 gms paneer - cut into 1" pieces
200 gm spring onions - cut white bulb into rings and cut greens diagonally into
½" pieces, keep greens separate
1 green chilli - deseeded & chopped
4 tbsp oil
6-8 flakes garlic - crushed
2 tomatoes - pureed in a mixer
2 tomatoes - finely chopped
1 tbsp tomato ketchup
3 laung (cloves) - crushed roughly
¼ tsp haldi, 2 tsp dhania (coriander) powder
1¼ tsp salt, or to taste, ½ tsp red chilli powder
½ tsp garam masala
4 tbsp fresh cream or ¼ cup milk

1. Cut white bulb of spring onion into rings and cut green part diagonally into ½" pieces.
2. Heat 4 tbsp oil in a kadhai. Add garlic. Saute for 1 minute on low flame. Add the white of onions and stir fry till light brown.
3. Add ¼ tsp haldi. Stir for 1 minute.
4. Add fresh tomato puree and chopped tomatoes and stir fry for 5-7 minutes, till they turn almost dry.
5. Add tomato ketchup. Stir to mix well.
6. Add crushed laung. Cook for ½ minute.
7. Reduce heat. Add dhania powder, salt, red chilli powder and garam masala. Cook for 2 minutes on low heat.
8. Add ¼ cup water. Boil. Add the paneer, greens of onions and chopped green chilli. Cook for 1-2 minutes on low flame till well mixed.
9. Keeping the heat low, add cream or milk. Mix. Remove from fire and serve hot.

Step 1

Step 4

Note: If spring onions are not available, use 1 capsicum cut into thin long pieces and 2 small, ordinary onions cut into thin rings.

Paneer Kadhai Waala

Dry fenugreek leaves as well as fenugreek seeds along with coriander seeds are the important ingredients of a kadhai masala. A little curd gives body to the dish.

Serves 4

200 gms paneer - cut into 1" cubes
4 onions - cut into rings
1 capsicum - cut into rings
6-7 flakes garlic - crushed
2" long, piece of ginger - cut into thin match sticks or grated
4 tbsp ready made tomato puree
1 cup thick curd - well beaten till smooth
2 tsp kasoori methi (dry fenugreek leaves)
1 tsp salt
2 pinches sugar
5 tbsp oil

KADHAI MASALA (ROAST TOGETHER & GRIND)
1½ tsp saboot dhania (coriander seeds)
1 tsp jeera (cumin seeds)
3 dry, red chillies
¼ tsp methi daana (fenugreek seeds)
4-5 saboot kali mirch (pepper corns)

1. Roast saboot dhania, jeera, red chillies, methi daana and saboot kali mirch on a tawa, on low flame for 4-5 minutes. Do not let the seeds turn brown. Cool and grind to a powder in a small spice grinder or on the chakla - belan.
2. Heat 3 tbsp oil in a kadhai. Add onion rings and cook till brown. Add capsicum. Stir fry for 2 minutes. Remove onion and capsicum from kadhai and keep aside.
3. Heat 2 tbsp oil in the kadhai. Add crushed garlic. Cook till light brown.

Step 6

4. Add powdered kadhai masala. Cook for ½ minute.
5. Add ginger.
6. Add tomato puree. Cook for 1 minute.
7. Reduce heat. Add curd gradually, stirring continuously. Add kasoori methi. Cook for 5-7 minutes on low heat.
8. Crumble 4-5 pieces of paneer & mix with the masala.
9. Add rest of paneer pieces, fried onions and capsicums.
10. Add salt & 2 pinches of sugar. Mix well. Remove after a few seconds. Serve hot.

Kasturi Paneer

Serves 4

1 packet (25 gms) kasoori methi (dried fenugreek leaves)
250 gms paneer - cut in tiny cubes (¼" pieces)
4 tbsp fresh malai or cream or ¼ cup milk
salt to taste, ¼ tsp haldi, ½ tsp red chilli powder

1. Clean methi. Remove stalks. Wash in plenty of water. Soak in water for 1 hour atleast or preferably for some more time. Squeeze and chop methi finely.
2. Heat oil in a kadhai and deep fry paneer cubes to a light golden colour.
3. Heat 4 tbsp oil. Add methi and fry in oil for 4-5 minutes.
4. Add salt, haldi and chilli powder. Add cream or milk and cook for 2 minutes.
5. Lastly add the lightly fried paneer. Mix well. Serve hot.

Quick Stir Fried Paneer

Serves 4

200 gm paneer - cut into fingers
½ tsp jeera (cumin seeds)
2 dry, red chillies - broken into pieces & deseeded
1 onion - sliced thinly
1 capsicum - deseeded & cut into thin fingers
1 tomato - cut into four lengthways, remove pulp and cut into thin long pieces
¼ tsp dhania (coriander) powder, ¼ tsp red chilli powder
¼ tsp garam masala, 1 tsp salt, or to taste
2 tbsp tomato puree
1 tbsp chopped green coriander
1" piece ginger - shredded or cut into match sticks

1. Slice onion, capsicum and tomato lengthwise.
2. Heat 3 tbsp oil in a kadhai. Reduce heat. Add jeera and red chillies. Let jeera turn golden.
3. Add onion and stir fry for a minute till slightly cooked.
4. Add the capsicum and stir for ½ minute.
5. Add dhania powder, red chill powder, garam masala and ½ tsp salt.
6. Add tomato puree and paneer. Mix well. Add ½ tsp salt on the paneer.
7. Add tomato slices, coriander and shredded ginger (or ginger match sticks). Mix and remove from heat. Serve hot.

Paneer Taka-Tak

Serves 4

**300 gms paneer (cottage cheese) slab - cut into 1" thick rectangle of size - 8" x 3"
approx. (get the paneer block cut horizontally when purchasing paneer)
2 capsicums
2 onions, 1 firm tomato**

MARINADE
**1 cup (200 gms) curd of full cream milk - hang for 15 minutes in a muslin cloth
¾ tsp salt, ½ tsp red chilli powder, 1 tbsp oil
a pinch of orange red colour**

DRY MASALA (GRIND TOGETHER)
**seeds of 5-6 chhoti illaichi (green cardamoms)
3-4 sticks of dalchini (cinnamon)
8-10 laung (cloves)
1 tsp ajwain (carom seeds)**

1. Mix all the ingredients of the marinade together, to get a bright orange colour.
2. Cover the paneer slab with this marinade, spreading on all the sides. Keep on a greased wire rack or grill.
3. Heat oven to 180°C. Grill paneer for 15 min or till the curd dries up and forms a coating. Keep a piece of aluminium foil beneath the wire rack to collect drippings.
4. Turn the paneer carefully when it appears dry. Keep it in the oven for 5-7 minutes if it is wet on the other side. Remove from oven and keep aside.
5. Cut capsicums into 8 pieces to get 1" pieces of capsicum. Cut onion into four pieces and separate the onion leaves. Cut tomatoes into 8 pieces. Remove pulp.
6. Heat 1½ tbsp oil in a non-stick pan or a tawa. Add 1 tsp of the freshly ground dry masala. Immediately put the slab of paneer. Cook on low heat for 1 minute. Do not let it turn black. Turn the slab again. Remove from pan. Keep aside.
7. To serve, keep the paneer covered with foil in a hot oven for 5-7 minutes till it gets soft and hot or microwave for 2 minutes covering with a cling wrap.
8. In the meantime, heat 2 tbsp oil in the pan, add 1 tsp dry masala powder, add the capsicum and onions immediately. Cook for 2-3 minutes. Add tomatoes, sprinkle ½ tsp salt on the vegetables. Mix well.
9. Place paneer in a platter. Cut diagonally into pieces, keeping the pieces joined together. Serve paneer surrounded by vegetables.

Paneer Do Pyaza

Serves 4

150 gms paneer - cut into finger shaped pieces
2 big onions - cut into slices
4 tbsp chopped fresh dhania (green coriander)
1 firm tomato - cut into 1" pieces
1 green chilli - finely cut lengthways
½" piece ginger - cut into thin long pieces
1½ tsp saboot dhania (coriander seeds) - crushed
¼ tsp garam masala, ¼ tsp red chilli powder, ½ tsp salt,

GRAVY
3 onions and 1" piece ginger - grind together
2 sticks dalchini (cinnamon), 5 tbsp oil
½ tsp salt, ¼ tsp haldi, 1 tsp dhania (coriander) powder
½ tsp red chilli powder, ½ tsp garam masala
seeds of 2 moti illaichi (big cardamom) - crushed on a chakla belan
½ cup curd

1. Cut tomato into half. Cut each half into 4 equal pieces. Remove pulp and keep pieces and pulp aside. Slice onions. Slit green chillies, deseed, and cut into long thin pieces. Crush saboot dhania on a chakla belan to a rough powder.
2. Heat 2 tbsp oil. Add sliced onions and stir-fry till they start turning brown. Add crushed dhania and cook for ½ minute.
3. Add garam masala, salt, and chilli powder. Mix well.
4. Add tomato pieces, green chilli, ginger and paneer.
5. Sprinkle hara dhania on the paneer. Mix gently. Stir for 1-2 minutes on low flame. Keep aside.
6. To prepare the gravy, grind 3 onions and 1" piece ginger together.
7. In a clean kadhai, heat 5 tbsp oil. Add dalchini. After ½ minute, add the onion paste. Stir fry till onions turn golden brown.
8. Add salt, haldi, dhania powder, red chilli powder and garam masala. Cook for a few seconds. Add the tomato pulp and cook for 2-3 minutes.
9. Beat curd with a spoon and add it gradually to the onion paste.
10. Cook for 10-15 minutes till the masala turns brown again and the oil separates.
11. Crush seeds of moti illaichi on chakla - belan and add to the masala. Cook for a few seconds.
12. Add enough hot water, about 1 cup, to get a thick masala gravy. Boil gravy. Simmer on low heat for 5 minutes.
13. Add the pyaz - paneer mixture prepared earlier. Mix gently. Remove from fire.

Tikka Paneer Subzi

A delightful paneer dish which is relished with meals as a side dish.

Serves 4

250 gms paneer - cut into 1" cubes
¾ tsp salt, ¼ tsp red chilli powder
¼ tsp haldi (turmeric powder) or a pinch of red colour
1 tsp lemon juice, 1 tbsp oil
2 capsicums - cut into fine rings
2 onions - cut into fine rings
¼ tsp kala namak (black salt)
¼ tsp salt
2 tsp tandoori masala

GRIND TO A ROUGH PASTE WITHOUT ANY WATER
1½" piece ginger, 2-3 green chillies
1 tsp jeera (cumin seeds)
3- 4 flakes garlic - optional

1. Cut capsicum and onion into fine rings.
2. Grind garlic, ginger, jeera and green chillies to a thick rough paste. Do not add water.
3. Add ¾ tsp salt, chilli powder and lemon juice to the paste. Add a little haldi or colour to give colour to the paste.
4. Cut paneer into 1" squares. Apply ¾ of this ginger-chilli paste nicely on all the pieces. Keep the left over paste aside.
5. Place this paneer on a greased wire rack of an oven and grill for 10-15 minutes till it is dry and slightly crisp. Keep aside till serving time.
6. At serving time, heat 1 tbsp oil in a kadhai. Fry onion and capsicum rings for a few minutes till onions turn transparent.
7. Add the left over ginger-chilli paste and a few drops of lemon juice. Add black salt and ¼ tsp salt too.
8. Add paneer pieces. Sprinkle tandoori masala. Toss for a minute till the paneer turns soft and is heated properly. Serve immediately.

Step 1

Step 4

Step 5

Paneer Amravati

Onion and coconut shreds coat paneer fingers in a South Indian style.

Serves 4-6

200 gm paneer - cut into thin fingers
5 onions - 2 grated and 3 sliced
½ cup curry leaves
1½ tsp brown small rai (mustard seeds)
½ cup fresh coconut - grated finely
1¼ tsp salt, or to taste
3 tbsp lemon juice (juice of 1 large lemon)
a pinch of tandoori red colour

RED CHILLI PASTE

4 Kashmiri dry, red chillies - deseeded and soaked in warm water for 10 minutes
1" piece ginger, 1 tbsp cashews (kaju)
3 tbsp curd, 2 tsp dhania powder (coriander powder)
2-3 laung (cloves), 6-7 saboot kali mirch (peppercorns)

1. Grate 2 onions.
2. Cut the other 3 onions into halves. Then cut each half widthwise into half-rings to get thin strips of onion.
3. Scrape brown skin of ¼ of a coconut & grate finely to get ½ cup grated coconut.
4. Drain the soaked red chillies. Add all other ingredients of the paste and grind to a smooth paste using a little water for grinding.
5. Heat 6 tbsp oil. Add rai. Let it splutter for a minute.
6. Add grated onions and curry leaves. Cook till onions turn light brown.
7. Add onion slices and cook for 3-4 minutes till soft.
8. Add coconut and cook on low heat for 5 minutes till crisp. Keep it spread out while cooking.
9. Add red chilli paste and stir fry for 2-3 minutes.
10. Add colour and salt.
11. Add 1 cup water. Boil.
12. Add paneer and mix well.
13. Cook on low heat for 5 minutes, stirring occasionaliy.
14. Add lemon juice and mix well. Serve hot.

Step 4

Step 6

Indian Meal Time Dishes
Gravies & Curries

**Scooping of Paneer, by making squares
with the help of a knife**

Broccoli Bonanza

Serves 4   Picture on page 30

250 gm paneer (take a square shaped whole block of paneer weighing 250 gms)
salt, red chilli powder and chat masala to sprinkle

CURRY
2 tbsp oil, 1 onion - sliced
2 tbsp curry powder (MDH), 2 tbsp finely chopped coriander
2 cups milk, 1 tsp salt, or to taste, 2 tsp cornflour mixed with 1 tbsp water

FILLING
½ cup grated broccoli, ½ tsp ginger- garlic paste, ½ of a small onion- chopped
½ tsp salt, ½ tsp pepper, ½ tsp tomato sauce

1. Cut paneer into 4 big pieces and then divide each piece to get 8 equal square pieces. With the help of a knife from the centre of each piece scoop out the paneer forming a square shaped hollow. Leave a border of ¼" all around. Do not dig very deep. Let the bottom be intact (see the lower picture on page 64). Keep the scooped out paneer aside.
2. Sprinkle salt, chilli powder and chat masala on all sides of paneer. Keep aside.
3. For the curry, heat 2 tbsp oil in a small, heavy pan. Reduce heat. Add onion and stir till golden. Add curry powder and fresh coriander and stir for a few seconds.
4. Add 2 tbsp of the crushed scooped paneer and 1 tsp salt. Mix well.
5. Remove pan from heat & add milk, stirring continuously. Return the pan to heat and stir until the sauce comes to a boil. Boil for 1 minute, stirring continuously.
6. Add cornflour mixed with water and stir for 2 minutes on low heat till slightly thick. Remove from fire. Keep curry aside.
7. For filling, heat 1 tbsp oil in a pan, add ginger- garlic paste. Wait for a minute.
8. Add onion and cook till golden. Add broccoli. Mix.
9. Add salt, pepper and tomato ketchup. Cook for a minute. Remove from fire.
10. Heat 2 tbsp oil in a pan. Fry gently 4 pieces of paneer blocks at a time. Fry turning all the sides till golden.
11. Remove on paper napkins. Fill 1 tsp of filling in each scooped out block.
12. In a shallow rectangular serving dish, put the hot gravy. Arrange the stuffed paneer blocks on the gravy. Cover and heat in an oven or a microwave. Serve.

Step 10

Note: If using a microwave, cover loosely with a cling film and micro high for 2 minutes. If using an ordinary oven, cover loosely with aluminium foil and heat for 5-8 minutes in a moderately hot oven at 180°C till hot.

Saunfiyaan Dhania Paneer

Picture on facing page   *Serves 4*

200 gms paneer - cut into 1" square pieces
2 tbsp kaju (cashewnuts) - soak in warm water for 10 minutes & grind to a paste
4 tbsp oil
1 big onion - finely chopped
1" piece ginger & 8-10 flakes garlic - crushed to a paste or 2 tsp ginger-garlic paste
½ tsp red chilli powder, ½ tsp garam masala
1 tsp salt, or to taste,
1 tsp dhania powder
2 tbsp chopped coriander
1 cup milk

CORIANDER PASTE
¾ cup chopped coriander
2 green chillies, 1 tbsp saunf (fennel)
½ cup milk

Step 2

1. Soak kaju in a little warm water for 10-15 minutes. Drain. Grind in a mixer blender to a very smooth paste using about 2 tbsp water.
2. Grind all the ingredients given under coriander paste to a thin paste in a mixer- grinder.
3. Heat 4 tbsp oil in a kadhai and add the chopped onions. Fry till golden.
4. Add the ginger- garlic paste, stir for few seconds.
5. Reduce heat, add the prepared coriander paste. Cook for 2 minutes.

Step 5

6. On medium flame, add red chilli powder, garam masala, salt and dhania powder.
7. Add the prepared kaju paste. Mix well. Keep scraping sides if masala sticks to the sides/ bottom of the kadhai. Stir till masala leaves oil.
8. Add ½ cup of water. Boil, stirring at intervals. Remove from fire. Let the gravy cool down a little.

Step 9

9. Add milk, mix well. Add paneer and return to fire and cook stirring continuously on low heat for 3- 4 minutes.
10. Serve hot, garnished with chopped coriander.

Lachhedar Paneer Crisps: Recipe on page 12, Saunfiyaan Dhania Paneer ➤

Rajasthani Bharwaan Lauki

Roundels of bottle gourd stuffed with paneer.

Serves 4-6   *Picture on opposite page*

500 gm lauki (bottle gourd) - choose lauki of medium thickness

FILLING
200 gm paneer - crumbled (mash roughly)
1 tsp finely chopped ginger, 1 green chilli - finely chopped
2 tbsp chopped green coriander
8-10 kaju (cashewnuts) - chopped
8-10 kishmish (raisins) - soaked in water
¾ tsp salt or to taste

MASALA
2 tbsp oil or ghee
2 laung (cloves), 2 tej patta (bay leaves)
seeds of 2 chhoti illaichi (green cardamoms)
1" stick dalchini (cinnamon)

TOMATO PASTE (Grind Together)
3 tomatoes
1 green chilli
½" piece ginger
½ tsp red chilli powder, 1 tsp dhania powder, ¼ tsp haldi, ¾ tsp salt
½ tsp jeera (cumin seeds), ¼ tsp sugar

1. Peel lauki. Cut vertically into two pieces from the centre to get 2 smaller pieces.
2. Boil in salted water, covered, for about 10 minutes, till done. Remove from water and cool.
3. Scoop seeds from both the pieces of the lauki and make them hollow.
4. For filling - Mix paneer, ginger, green chilli, coriander, kaju, kishmish and salt.
5. Stuff it into the boiled lauki pieces. Keep aside.
6. For masala- heat ghee. Add laung, illaichi, seeds of chhoti illaichi, dalchini and tej patta. Stir for a minute.
7. Add the prepared tomato paste. Stir for 3-4 minutes till thick and oil separates.
8. Add 1½ cups water. Boil. Simmer for 4-5 minutes till oil separates. Keep aside.
9. At serving time, saute whole lauki pieces in a non stick pan in 1 tbsp oil, turning sides carefully to brown from all sides. Remove from pan.
10. Pour half of the hot gravy in a dish. Cut the lauki into ¾" thick round pieces and arrange over the gravy. Pour the remaining hot tomato gravy on top. Serve.

Mewa Seekh in Gravy

Do not get put off by the long list of ingredients, the final product is delicious. The seekhs are simple to make and the ingredients are easily available! The gravy can also be used with simply fried paneer, or baby corns or any koftas.

Picture on page 1   Serves 4

¾ cups grated paneer (75 gms)
a few toothpicks
¼ cup dry bread crumbs
1 tsp cornflour
¼ tsp garam masala, ¼- ½ tsp salt or to taste

DRY ROAST ON A TAWA
1 tsp chironji (sunflower seeds)
1 tsp magaz (melon seeds)

PASTE (GRIND TOGETHER)
½" piece ginger, 3-4 flakes garlic
1 green chilli
3 tbsp green coriander
5 kaju (cashewnuts), 4 badam (almonds)
3 kishmish (raisins), 2- 3 whole pistas (pistachio)
¼ tsp jaiphal (nutmeg)
¼ tsp javetri (mace)

GRAVY
2 onions, ½" piece of ginger and 3- 4 flakes of garlic - ground to a paste
1 tsp ginger-garlic paste
4 tbsp kasoori methi (dry fenugreek leaves)
½ cup fresh cream or thin malai
3 tbsp oil
1 tbsp butter
1 tsp salt, or to taste, ½ tsp red chilli powder
½ tsp garam masala, a pinch of amchoor
1 cup milk (approx.)

POWDER (GRIND TOGETHER)
½" stick dalchini (cinnamon)
seeds of 2-3 chhoti illaichi (green cardamom)
3-4 laung (cloves)
4-5 saboot kali mirch (peppercorns)
2 tbsp cashewnuts (kaju)

Contd...

1. Roast magaz and chironji on a tawa on low heat. Cool.

Step 1

2. Grind all the ingredients given under paste in a mixer to a paste.

3. Mix together - ¼ cup bread crumbs, cornflour, garam masala, salt, grated paneer, roasted chironji, magaz, and the prepared paste. Mix well.

4. Take a lemon sized ball of the mixture. Make a small roll of 1½" length. Flatten it from the sides. Insert a toothpick from one flattened end to the other, going straight out of the roll, without puncturing the roll at any other point. Repeat with the left over mixture. Keep the seekhs covered with a cling wrap in the refrigerator for atleast ½ hour so that they get set properly.

Step 4

5. Grind all the ingredients given under powder together on a chakla belan or in a small spice grinder. Keep aside the powder.

6. For the gravy, heat 3 tbsp oil and 1 tbsp butter. Add onion-garlic paste and cook on low heat till oil separates. Do not let the onions turn brown.

Step 7

7. Add the freshly ground masala-kaju powder. Cook for a few seconds.

8. Add kasoori methi and cream, cook on low heat for 2-3 minutes till cream dries up.

9. Add salt, red chilli powder, garam masala and amchoor. Stir for 1 minute.

10. Add 1 cup milk and ½ cup water. Boil for 1 minute on low heat. Remove from fire.

11. Heat oil in a kadhai. Remove seekhs from the fridge. Deep fry the seekhs one at a time alongwith the toothpicks till golden brown. Drain on paper napkins. Keep aside till serving time.

12. At serving time, heat sticks and gravy separately. Pour the hot gravy in a serving dish and arrange the hot sticks over it. If you want, put some gravy in the serving dish, arrange seekhs and again pour the rest of the gravy on top. If you like, you can heat the seekhs in gravy together, in a microwave. Serve hot.

Anaari Paneer Khumb

Red pomegranates and paneer stuffed in mushrooms and put in a cardamom flavoured yellow gravy!

Serves 6-8

200 gm mushrooms (12-15 big size pieces)
juice of ½ lemon, 2 tsp salt
1 cup red kandhari anaar ke dane (fresh red pomegranate)

FILLING
50 gms paneer - grated (½ cup)
1 small onion - chopped, ½" piece ginger- grated
1 tbsp kaju (cashewnuts) - crushed on a chakla belan
3 tbsp anaar ke dane, 3 tbsp chopped coriander
½ tsp garam masala, ½ tsp black pepper
½ tsp bhuna jeera powder (roasted cumin), 2-3 big pinches of salt

GRAVY
3 onions, 1½" piece ginger, 4 dry red chillies
4 tbsp oil
4-5 chhoti illaichi (green cardamoms) - pounded to open slightly
½ tsp garam masala, ½ tsp red chilli powder, ½ tsp haldi
1 tsp dhania powder, 1½ tsp salt or to taste
1 cup milk, 1 tbsp finely chopped coriander

1. Wash mushrooms and pull out the stalks. Hollow the mushrooms a little more with the help of a small scooper. Keep stalks aside.

2. Boil 4-5 cups water with juice of ½ lemon and 2 tsp salt.

3. Add the mushrooms. Boil for 2 minutes. Drain and refresh with cold water. Strain. Wipe to dry well.

4. For filling- heat oil in a kadhai, add onion, cook till soft. Add all the other ingredients given under filling. Mix well.

Step 1

5. Stuff each mushroom with it. Place the mushrooms in a hot oven at 200°C for 3-4 minutes. Remove from oven and keep aside.

6. To prepare the gravy, blend the anaar ke daane with 1½ cups water in a mixer blender. Strain to get juice.

Contd...

7. Trim the left over mushroom stalks. Grind mushroom stalks with onions, ginger and dry red chillies to a fine paste.
8. Heat 4 tbsp oil in a heavy kadhai. Add chhoti illaichi. Wait for a minute.
9. Add the onion-mushroom paste. Cook on low flame for about 7-8 minutes till onions turn light brown.
10. Add garam masala, red chilli powder, haldi, dhania and salt.
11. Add anaar ka ras. Boil, simmer for 5 minutes.
12. Reduce heat. Add milk to the gravy. Boil on low heat. Simmer on low flame for 5 minutes without covering. Keep aside.
13. To serve, boil gravy. Pour in a serving dish. Arrange mushrooms on it. Heat in a microwave or an oven. Serve immediately, sprinkled with coriander and kaju.

Methi Malai Paneer

Shreds of dry fenugreek leaves (kasoori methi) make this white curry really appetizing.

Serves 4

200 gms paneer (cottage cheese) - cut into small, ½" cubes
½ cup shelled, boiled peas
1 tbsp cashewnuts (kaju) - grind to a fine powder
1 onion - ground to a paste
¼ tsp pepper powder, preferably white pepper
½ cup (75 gms) malai (cream) - whip with ½ cup milk till smooth
4 tbsp kasoori methi (dry fenugreek leaves)
salt to taste, a pinch of sugar, ½ cup milk (approx.)

CRUSH TOGETHER
½ stick dalchini (cinnamon), 3-4 laung (cloves), 2 moti illaichi (cardamoms)

1. Crush together dalchini, laung and seeds of moti illaichi on a chakla-belan. Keep the masala aside.
2. Heat 2 tbsp oil. Add onion paste and cook on low heat till oil separates. Do not let the onion turn brown.

Step 2

3. Add the crushed spices and pepper powder. Cook for a few seconds.
4. Add kasoori methi and malai, cook on low heat for 2-3 minutes till malai dries up slightly.
5. Add boiled peas and paneer.
6. Add powdered kajus and cook for a few seconds.
7. Add enough milk to get a thick gravy. Add salt and sugar to taste. Bring to a boil.
8. Serve garnished with some kajus roasted on a tawa till golden.

Aneez Paneer

Serves 4-6

200 gm paneer - cut into 1½" long pieces
2 tbsp kaju (cashewnuts) - soaked in warm water for 10 min & ground to a paste
4 tbsp oil
1 large onion - finely chopped
1" piece ginger and 8-10 flakes garlic - crushed to a paste (2½ tsp paste)
½ tsp pepper, ½ tsp garam masala
¼ tsp dhania powder, 1 tsp salt, or to taste,
1½ tbsp kasoori methi (dry fenugreek leaves)
¼ cup grated cheddar cheese (cheese tin or cubes) - grated
½ cup milk
¼ cup cream

GARNISH
1 tbsp kishmish and some grated cheese (optional)

1. Soak kaju in a little warm water for 10-15 minutes.
2. Drain kaju. Grind in a mixer blender to a very smooth paste using about 2 tbsp water. Keep aside.

Step 2

Step 2

4. Heat oil in a kadhai and add the chopped onion. Fry till golden.
5. Add the ginger- garlic paste. Saute for ½ a minute.
6. Reduce heat, add pepper, garam masala, dhania powder, salt, kasoori methi, cheese and kaju paste. Cook for 2 minutes.
7. Add ½ cup of water and cheese. Boil. Remove from fire. Let the gravy cool down a little.
8. Add milk, 1 cup water and cream to the cooled gravy. Return to fire and stirring continuously on low heat, cook for 2-3 minutes.
9. Add paneer and cook for a minute. Serve hot garnished with kishmish.

Step 8

Step 9

Piste Waala Paneer

A rich Mughlai style of cooking paneer with pista paste, giving the curry a lovely green colour and flavour.

Serves 6

300 gm paneer - cut into 1" squares
2 large onions
½ cup curd - beat well till smooth
2 tsp ginger-garlic paste or 1" ginger piece & 4-5 flakes garlic - crushed to a paste
1 tbsp dhania powder, 1 tsp salt, or to taste
½ tsp pepper powder, preferably white pepper powder
½ cup fresh cream
½ tsp garam masala powder

GRIND TOGETHER TO A PASTE WITH ¼ CUP WATER
½ cup pistas (pistachio nuts) with the hard cover- skinned, soaked and peeled
1 green chilli - finely chopped
¼ cup chopped fresh coriander

1. Peel and cut onions into 4 pieces. Boil in 1 cup water for 2-3 minutes. Drain, cool slightly and grind to a fine paste. Keep boiled onion paste aside.
2. Cut paneer into 1" pieces.
3. Soak pista in hot water for 10 minutes, drain and peel. Reserve a few peeled pistachio nuts for garnish.

Step 2

4. Grind remaining peeled pistas with chopped green chillies & coriander to a fine green paste with ¼ cup water.
5. Heat 4 tbsp oil in a kadhai, add boiled onion paste and saute for 7-8 minutes on low heat till dry and oil separates. See that the colour of the onions does not change to brown.
6. Add ginger-garlic paste and stir-fry for a minute.
7. Add dhania powder, pepper powder and salt and mix well.

Step 10

8. Stir in the pista-green chilli paste and cook for 2 minutes on low heat.
9. Add 1½ cups water & simmer on low heat for 2-3 minutes.
10. Add curd, simmer for 1 minute, stirring continuously.
11. Stir in fresh cream, sprinkle garam masala powder and transfer to a serving dish. Sprinkle remaining pistachio nuts and some cream. Serve hot.

Paneer Makhani

Picture on facing page   Serves 4

250 gm paneer - cut into 1" cubes
5 large (500 gm) tomatoes - each cut into 4 pieces
2 tbsp desi ghee or butter and 2 tbsp oil
4-5 flakes garlic and 1" piece ginger - ground to a paste (1½ tsp ginger-garlic paste)
1 tbsp kasoori methi (dry fenugreek leaves), 1 tsp tomato ketchup
½ tsp jeera (cumin seeds), 2 tsp dhania powder, ½ tsp garam masala
1 tsp salt, or to taste, ½ tsp red chilli powder, preferably degi mirch
½ cup water, ½-1 cup milk, approx., ½ cup cream (optional)
3 tbsp cashewnuts (kaju)

1. Soak kaju in a little warm water for 10-15 minutes.

Step 1   Step 2

2. Drain kaju. Grind in a mixer to a very smooth paste using about 2 tbsp water.
3. Boil tomatoes in ½ cup water. Simmer for 4-5 minutes on low heat till tomatoes turn soft. Remove from fire and cool. Grind the tomatoes along with the water to a smooth puree.
4. Heat oil and ghee or butter in a kadhai. Reduce heat. Add jeera. When it turns golden, add ginger-garlic paste.
5. When paste starts to change colour add the above tomato puree & cook till dry.
6. Add kasoori methi and tomato ketchup.
7. Add masalas - dhania powder, garam masala, salt and red chilli powder. Mix well for a few seconds. Cook till oil separates.
8. Add cashew paste. Mix well for 2 minutes.
9. Add water. Boil. Simmer on low heat for 4-5 minutes. Reduce heat.
10. Add the paneer cubes. Remove from fire. Keep aside to cool for about 5 minutes.
11. Add enough milk to the cold paneer masala to get a thick curry, mix gently. (Remember to add milk only after the masala is no longer hot, to prevent the milk from curdling. After adding milk, heat curry on low heat.)
12. Heat on low heat, stirring continuously till just about to boil.
13. Add cream, keeping the heat very low and stirring continuously. Remove from fire immediately and transfer to a serving dish. Swirl 1 tbsp cream over the hot paneer in the dish. Serve immediately.

Variation:

For dakshini tadka, heat 1 tbsp oil. Add ½ tsp rai. After 30 seconds add 4-5 curry leaves. Stir. Remove from fire. Add a pinch of red chilli powder and pour over the hot paneer makhani in the dish.

Dum Paneer Kali Mirch

Dum - The Avadh way to flavour the cooked dish. At the end of cooking, flavourful spices are added to the dish. The dish is sealed with dough or a very tight fitting lid and kept on very low heat in the oven or on fire, for the vegetable, meat or paneer to absorb the exotic flavour of the spice added. Here black peppercorns lend their flavour to paneer.

Serves 6   *Picture on opposite page*

300 gms paneer - cut into 1" cubes
½ cup fresh coriander leaves
¼ cup fresh mint leaves - finely chopped
1 cup yogurt (curd) - beat till smooth
2 tbsp desi ghee
2 tej patta (bay leaves), 1" stick dalchini (cinnamon)
3-4 chhoti illaichi (green cardamoms), 3-4 laung (cloves)
2 tbsp dhania powder (ground coriander), 1 tsp jeera powder, 1½ tsp salt or to taste

DUM INGREDIENTS
1 level tbsp saboot kali mirch (peppercorns) - crushed in a spice grinder
½ cup fresh cream, ½ tsp garam masala

PASTE
2-3 green chillies, 1" piece ginger - chopped, 4-5 flakes garlic
4 onions - sliced and deep fried till golden

1. For paste- finely slice the onions. Heat oil in a kadhai and deep fry the sliced onions in hot oil till golden brown. Drain on an absorbent paper napkin and cool.
2. Grind the fried onions along with garlic, ginger and green chillies with ¼ cup water to a smooth paste. Keep aside onion- garlic paste.
3. Heat desi ghee in a narrow-mouthed handi or a pan with a well fitting lid.
4. Add tej patta, dalchini, chhoti illaichi and laung. Wait for ½ minute.
5. Add onion-garlic paste and saute for 2 minutes on low heat.
6. Reduce heat. Add the beaten yogurt. Mix well.
7. Add dhania powder, jeera powder and salt to taste. Stir for 2 minutes. Add 2 cups water and bring to a boil.
8. Add the paneer pieces and mix in the chopped coriander and mint leaves.
9. Stir in the fresh cream and crushed black peppercorns. Sprinkle garam masala.
10. Cover the handi with a tight-fitting lid and seal using whole wheat flour (atta dough) or alternately, seal tightly with aluminium foil.
11. Preheat oven to 180°C. Place sealed handi in the preheated oven or on a tawa on very low flame and cook for 10-15 minutes. Open the handi just before serving and serve immediately.

Kashmiri Bharwaan Aloo

Serves 4- 6

4 medium round potatoes, 3 tbsp maida, oil for frying

FILLING

**100 gms *paneer* (cottage cheese), 1 small onion - finely chopped
2 tsp kaju (cashewnuts) - chopped, 1 tsp kishmish (raisins)- chopped
1 green chilli - chopped finely, 1 tbsp oil, salt to taste**

GRAVY

**3 tbsp oil, 4 tbsp very finely grated khoya (about 50 gm)
1½ tbsp kasoori methi (dry fenugreek leaves), 1½ tsp salt or to taste
½ tsp garam masala, 1 tej patta, 1 tsp shah jeera (royal cumin)**

ONION PASTE

**1 onion, 2 laung, seeds of 2 chhoti illaichi, 2 tbsp saunf
¾" piece of ginger, 4- 5 flakes of garlic, seeds of 2 moti illaichi, 1" stick dalchini**

TOMATO PASTE

4 tomatoes - blanched and pureed in a mixer, ¼ tsp jaiphal, ¼ tsp javitri

KAJU PASTE

2½ tbsp kaju (cashewnuts), 2 dry, red chillies, 2 tbsp khus- khus (poppy seeds)

Step 1 **Step 2**

1. Peel, wash potatoes. Prick with a fork. Cut into 2 pieces widthwise.
2. Scoop out the inner portion.
3. Keep the potatoes in salted water for 15 minutes. Strain and pat dry.
4. Heat oil and deep fry all the potatoes together. Fry on medium heat till the potatoes get cooked properly and are golden brown in colour. Take out one piece from oil and check. If ready then remove all the pieces from kadhai on paper napkins. Keep aside.
5. For filling, heat oil. Add onion and green chilli. Cook till onion turns light pink.
6. Add kaju and kishmish. Cook for 1 minute.
7. Add crumbled paneer and salt. Cook for a few seconds. Remove from fire. Cool.
8. Fill the potatoes with the prepared filling. Press to level it.
9. Spread maida in a flat plate, invert the potato with the filling side down on the maida.
10. Heat 2 tbsp oil in a pan, put potatoes with the filling side down in oil. Fry on medium flame till maida forms a crisp coating over the filling. Remove from fire.

10. For gravy, grind all the ingredients of onion paste to a smooth paste.
11. Grind all the ingredients of tomato paste to a smooth paste. Keep aside.
12. Grind all the ingredients of kaju paste to a smooth paste. Keep aside.
13. For masala - heat 3 tbsp oil add tej patta and shah jeera, wait for a minute.
14. Add onion paste. Cook for 2- 3 minutes or till golden brown.
15. Add tomato paste. Stir for 3- 4 minutes or till oil separates.
16. Add kaju paste, salt and garam masala. Cook stirring for 2 minutes.
17. Add kasoori methi and finely grated khoya. Cook for 2 minutes, stirring.
18. Add 1 cup milk and ¾ cup of water. Boil. Add the fried potatoes. Cook for 2-3 minutes. Serve.

Paneer & Vegetable Korma

Serves 4

250 gm paneer - cut into 1" rectangular pieces and fried till golden
½ cup shelled peas
2 slices of tinned pineapple - cut into 1" pieces
2 small carrots - cut into round slices
4-5 french beans - cut into ½" diagonal pieces
2 onions - chopped finely, 4 tbsp oil
¼ tsp haldi (turmeric) powder, ½ tsp garam masala, 2 tsp salt

GRIND TOGETHER (CASHEW-CURD PASTE)
4 tsp khus-khus (poppy seeds) - soaked in warm water for 30 minutes and drained
¾ cup curd, 2 tbsp cashews (kaju)
2 tbsp grated coconut (fresh or desiccated)
2 whole dry red chillies, ½" piece ginger, 3-4 flakes garlic
2 tsp saboot dhania saboot, seeds of 2-3 chhoti illaichi (green cardamom)

1. Soak khus-khus and drain. Grind it along with kaju, coconut, red chillies, ginger, garlic, saboot dhania and chhoti illaichi together to a paste along with curd.
2. Cut paneer into 1" cubes and deep fry till golden.
3. Heat 4 tbsp oil. Add chopped onions. Cook till onions turn golden. Add haldi. Stir to mix well.
4. Add kaju paste. Cook on low heat for 3-4 minutes.
5. Add beans, peas and carrots. Stir for 2 minutes.
6. Add 1 cup water or enough to get a thick gravy. Boil.
7. Add garam masala and salt. Simmer for 5 minutes.
8. Add paneer and pineapple. Boil for 1 minute. Serve.

Step 2

Tirangana Paneer ka Salan

Three different coloured capsicums - red, yellow and green are used in the dish. If coloured capsicums are not available, you can use only green ones and add long, thin deseeded tomato pieces to add colour to the dish.

Serves 6

200 gm paneer - cut into thin, 1½" long fingers
½ green capsicum - cut into thin long pieces
½ red capsicum - cut into thin long pieces
½ yellow capsicum - cut into thin long pieces
4 tbsp oil, 1 tsp sarson (mustard seeds)
2 tbsp curry leaves, 2 onions - grated
a lemon sized ball of tamarind (imli) - soaked in ½ cup warm water
1½ tsp salt, or to taste, ½ tsp haldi (turmeric powder)

MASALA PASTE
½ cup roasted peanuts, 1" piece ginger - chopped, 6-8 flakes garlic - chopped

DRY ROAST ON A TAWA
2 tbsp til (sesame seeds), 1 tbsp saboot dhania (coriander seeds)
1 tsp jeera (cumin seeds), 2 dry, red chillies

Step 1

1. Mash soaked imli & strain to get imli pulp. Keep aside.
2. Sprinkle some salt, pepper and a pinch of haldi on the paneer. Mix well.
3. Heat 1 tbsp oil in a pan and rotate the pan to oil the bottom of the pan. Add the paneer pieces and saute the slices till golden. Remove from pan and add capsicums. Reduce heat and stir for 1 minute. Remove from pan and keep aside.
4. Dry roast sesame seeds, coriander seeds, cumin seeds and dry red chillies on a tawa till sesame seeds change colour.
5. Grind together all the ingredients of the masala paste, roasted seeds and dry red chilli to a paste with ¼ cup water.

Step 5

6. Heat oil add sarson, let it crackle and add curry leaves.
7. Add grated onion. Saute until onion is light golden brown, stirring continuously. Add haldi powder and mix well.
8. Add masala paste and stir.
9. Stir in 2 cups of water and bring it to a boil. Reduce the heat and cook covered for 5-7 minutes. Add salt and imli pulp to taste.
10. Add paneer and capsicums and cook on low heat for 1-2 minutes.

Pepper Paneer Chettinad

The fiery, delicious, brown curry of Chettinad - a place in South India.

Serves 4-6

250 gm paneer - cut into 1½" pieces & fried till golden
1 tbsp khus khus (poppy seeds)
2 tbsp cashewnuts (kaju)
4 tbsp oil
1 large onion - finely chopped
3 tomatoes - chopped
10-12 curry patta
1½ tsp salt, or to taste, ½ tsp haldi, 1 tsp chilli powder
1" piece ginger, 8-10 flakes garlic
1 tbsp lemon juice or to taste

CHETTINAD MASALA (ROASTED & GROUND)
½ cup freshly grated coconut (remove brown skin before grating)
1 tsp saboot dhania (coriander seeds)
1" dalchini (cinnamon stick)
½ tsp jeera (cumin seeds), 1 tsp saunf (fennel)
2-3 dry, whole red chillies
seeds of 3 chhoti illaichi (green cardamoms), 2-3 laung (cloves)

1. Soak khus khus and cashewnuts in a little warm water for 10-15 minutes.
2. Heat 1 tbsp oil in a kadhai or tawa. Add all ingredients of the chettinad masala. Stir-fry for 3-4 minutes till fragrant and golden. Remove from fire.
3. Drain khus and cashews. Grind together the roasted masala with the drained khus-khus-cashewnuts, ginger and garlic in a mixer blender to a very smooth paste using about ½ cup water.

Step 3

4. Heat oil in a kadhai and add the chopped onions. Fry till golden.
5. Add the ground paste and curry leaves. Saute for ½ a minute.
6. Add the chopped tomatoes, salt, haldi & chilli powder. Cook for about 10 minutes on medium flame, stirring in between till tomatoes are well blended.
7. Add lemon juice and 1½ cups of water. Boil. Simmer for 5-7 minutes. If you desire a thinner gravy, add some more water and give 3-4 quick boils.
8. Add fried paneer and boil. Simmer for 2-3 minutes. Garnish with coriander and some freshly ground pepper.

Haryali Paneer Kofta

Mouth-melting soft koftas with a crunchy nutty filling in green spinach gravy.

Serves 4

KOFTE
100 gm paneer, 1½ tbsp cornflour
¼ tsp roasted jeera (cumin seeds) powder, ¼ tsp red chilli powder, ¼ tsp salt
2 tbsp maida (plain flour) - to coat

FILLING
3-4 badaam (almonds) - chopped, 10-12 kishmish (raisins)
1 tsp very finely chopped ginger

GRAVY
250 gm paalak (spinach) - chopped (2½ cups)
2 green chillies - chopped
2 onions - ground to a paste
¼ cup ready-made tomato puree
1" piece ginger - crushed to a paste
5-7 flakes garlic - crushed to a paste
3 tbsp desi ghee or 4 tbsp oil
¼ tsp haldi powder, ½ tsp garam masala, ½ tsp salt, or to taste

1. Grate paneer. Mix paneer, cornflour, jeera powder, red chilli powder and salt.
2. Mix all ingredients of the filling together.
3. Make 8 marble sized balls. Stuff a bit of nuts in each ball. Roll in dry maida and deep fry one at a time to a light golden colour. Keep aside.
4. Discard stems of paalak leaves. Wash leaves in lots of water to remove grains of sand or soil. Pressure cook with ¼ cup water to give one whistle. Keep on low flame for 5-7 minutes. Remove from fire. Cool. Grind along with green chillies in a mixer.
5. Heat ghee and add onion paste. Fry till golden in colour.
6. Add tomato puree and cook on low flame for 2 minutes.
7. Add ginger and garlic paste. Cook for ½ minute.
8. Add haldi, garam masala and salt. Stir for 1 minute.
9. Add ground paalak and cook for 1 minute.
10. Add 2 cups hot water to get a thin green gravy. Boil. Keep on low flame for 10-15 minutes.
11. At serving time, add paneer koftas. Keep on low flame for 1 minute. Serve hot.

Step 6

Mughlai Dhingri Curry

Dhingri is a type of dried mushroom.It makes a great combination with paneer.

Serves 6

200 gms paneer (cottage cheese)
1 cup dhingri - soak for 2-3 hours in warm water
4 onions - sliced finely
10-12 kaju & 1 tbsp khus-khus (poppy seeds) - soak for 15 minutes in warm water
¼ cup fresh curd - well beaten
2 tomatoes - blanched and pureed
seeds of 2-3 chhoti illaichi (green cardamom) - powdered
1½ cup milk, ½-¾ cup water (approx.)
4 tbsp, 2 tbsp oil (6 tbsp)
1¼ tsp salt, or to taste, ¾ tsp red chilli powder
¼ tsp garam masala, ¼ tsp pepper
oil for deep frying

Step 1

1. Soak dhingri for 2- 3 hours in warm water. Wash it in several changes of water, scrubbing it well to remove dirt. Discard the hard stalks if any. Cut into small pieces as shown.
2. Soak khus-khus and kaju in ¼ cup water for 15 minutes.
3. Put tomatoes in boiling water for 2 minutes. Remove from water and peel the skin. Grind to a puree.

Step 3

4. Cut paneer into rectangular pieces of about ½" thickness. Heat oil and deep fry the paneer to a light golden colour. Keep aside.
5. Heat 4 tbsp oil and fry onions till they turn golden brown.
6. Remove from fire. Cool. Grind to a brown paste.
7. Grind soaked kaju and khus-khus to a white paste.
8. Heat 2 tbsp oil. Add the onion paste and cook on low heat till golden brown.
9. Add beaten curd and cook till the paste turns brown again. (3-4 minutes).
10. Add the blanched, pureed tomatoes. Cook till oil separates.
11. Add the soaked dhingri and stir fry for 2-3 minutes.
12. Add kaju-khus- khus paste and illaichi powder. Cook on low heat for 2 minutes.
13. Add milk and enough water to get a thick gravy.
14. Add salt, pepper, red chilli powder and garam masala. Boil the gravy and simmer for 2-3 minutes. Add the fried paneer. Let it come to a boil again. Serve hot.

Manzil-e-Paneer

Picture on facing page   Serves 8

700-800 gm paneer - cut into a long, thick slab (7" long and 2" thick, approx.)
salt, red chilli powder, haldi and chat masala to sprinkle, 2-3 tbsp grated cheese

FILLING (MIX TOGETHER)
½ cup grated carrot (½ carrot), ¼ cup chopped coriander
4-5 tbsp grated mozzarella or pizza cheese
¼ tsp salt and ¼ tsp freshly ground pepper, ½ tsp oregano, or to taste

TOMATO SAUCE
5 tomatoes - chopped roughly & boiled with ½ cup water
6 tbsp ready made tomato puree, 3 tbsp cream, 2 tbsp oil, 1 tsp crushed garlic
(6-8 flakes), ½ tsp black pepper, ½ tsp salt and ¼ tsp pepper, or to taste

GARNISH
a few capsicum strips and tomato pieces, some black pepper, 1 tbsp grated cheese

1. To prepare the sauce, boil chopped tomatoes in ½ cup water. Keep on low heat for 4-5 minutes till soft. Remove from fire. Mash and strain. Discard the skin. Keep fresh tomato puree aside.

2. Heat 2 tbsp oil. Reduce heat. Add garlic and stir till it just starts to change colour. Add 6 tbsp ready-made tomato puree. Cook till oil separates, for about 2-3 minutes on medium flame. Add the prepared fresh tomato puree and give one boil. Simmer on low heat for 5-6 minutes. Remove from fire. Let it cool.

3. Mix in cream. Add salt and pepper to taste and keep the sauce aside.

4. Cut paneer into 3 equal pieces lengthwise, getting big pieces of about ½" thick slices. Do not make them too thick. Sprinkle salt, red chilli powder, haldi and chat masala on both sides of each slice of paneer. Saute in 2 tbsp oil in a nonstick pan, changing sides carefully, till golden on both sides.

5. In a shallow rectangular serving dish, put ¼ of the prepared tomato sauce.

6. Place a paneer slab on the sauce.

7. Spread ½ of the carrot filling on it. Press another piece of paneer on it.

8. Again put the filling on it. Cover with the last piece of paneer. Press.

9. Pour the sauce all over the paneer to cover the top and the sides completely. Grate cheese on top. Garnish with tomatoes and capsicum. Sprinkle some pepper.

10. If using a microwave, cover loosely with a cling film and micro high for 2 minutes. If using an ordinary oven, cover loosely with aluminium foil and heat for 8-10 minutes in a moderately hot oven at 180°C till hot.

Shahi Paneer Kheer with Lychees or Fruit Balls: Recipe on page 122, Manzil-e-Paneer ➤

Paneer in Coconut Curry

Serves 4-6

300 gms paneer- cut into 1½" pieces

GRIND TO A PASTE
½ cup + 2 tbsp coconut - grated freshly
8 dry, red chillies - broken and deseeded
1 tsp jeera (cumin seeds)
1 tbsp saboot dhania (coriander seeds)
a pinch of haldi (turmeric powder)
a small lemon size ball of imli (tamarind) - deseeded
1" piece ginger, 5-6 flakes garlic

OTHER INGREDIENTS
1 onion - chopped
2 tomatoes - chopped, ½ tsp salt or to taste
2 cups coconut milk (readymade, tetra pack) or 1 packet coconut milk powder
(maggi) mixed with 2 cups of water

BATTER
½ cup besan, 3 tbsp chopped coriander
½ tsp each of salt, garam masala & pepper

1. Grind coconut, dry red chillies, jeera, saboot dhania, haldi, imli, ginger, garlic and ½ cup water to a paste. Keep coconut paste aside.
2. Heat 4-5 tbsp oil in a kadhai. Add the onion and saute till golden brown.
3. Add the tomatoes and cook for 5-6 minutes or till oil separates.
4. Add the ground coconut paste, cook on slow fire for 8-10 minutes.
5. Add coconut milk. Boil, stirring in between. Add salt to taste. Remove from fire.
6. Mix all the ingredients given under batter with about ¼ cup water to get a thick batter. Dip the paneer pieces in this batter and deep fry to a golden colour.
7. At the time of serving, add the fried paneer to the gravy and heat thoroughly.

Step 1   *Step 2*   *Step 5*

◄ *Paneer Jalfrezi: Recipe on page 54*

Butter Paneer Masala

Onion and capsicum rings with paneer in a red makhani gravy.

Serves 4-5

250 gms paneer (cottage cheese) - cut into 1½" cubes
1 tbsp kaju (cashewnuts) - powdered
4 big (250 gms) tomatoes - pureed
2 tsp kasoori methi (dry fenugreek leaves)
½ cup (100 ml) milk
¾ tsp bhuna jeera (roasted cumin seeds) powder
1 tsp red chilli powder, ½ tsp garam masala
1½ tsp salt, or to taste, ¼ - ½ tsp sugar
1 green chilli - slit lengthwise
1 big capsicum - cut into rings
2 onions - cut into thin rings
2 tbsp butter
few drops orange colour

PASTE
2 onions - chopped, 1" piece ginger - chopped, 6-7 flakes garlic

1. Cut capsicum and onion into rings. Keep aside.
2. Grind onions, ginger and garlic together to a paste.
3. Grind tomatoes to a puree.
4. Heat 5 tbsp oil in a kadhai, add onion paste in oil, till golden (on the lighter side). Do not make it brown.
5. Add kaju powdered in a small spice grinder. Cook for 2-3 minutes.
6. Add tomatoes. Cook for 10-15 minutes on low flame till oil separates. Add bhuna jeera powder, red chilli powder, garam masala, salt and sugar.
7. Add enough water, about 1½ cups. Cook for another 10-12 minutes till the oil separates and the gravy dries up to a thick masala gravy.
8. Add kasoori methi and milk. Cook on low flame for 2 minutes, stirring continuously. Remove from fire.
9. Heat butter in a clean kadhai, add green chillies, capsicum and onions. Saute for 2-3 minutes.
10. Add these vegetables, paneer and colour to the prepared gravy.
11. Return to fire, cook for another 2-3 minutes, stirring continuously. Serve hot.

Step 1

Step 5

Chinese
&
Thai

Nutty Saucy Paneer

Serves 4

250 gms paneer - cut into 1" cubes
1 small flower of broccoli (150 gms) - cut into 1" florets with very little stem
1 large onion - cut into 1" pieces
1 large tomato - remove pulp and cut into 1" pieces
5- 6 roasted kajus (cashewnuts) or regular kajus roasted on a tawa
6-7 flakes garlic - crushed and chopped
2 green chillies - chopped finely
3 tbsp oil
1 tbsp soya sauce
a dash of tabasco or capsico sauce
1 tbsp chilli garlic sauce
1 tbsp tomato ketchup
½ tsp salt, or to taste, ½ tsp pepper

1. Roast kaju on a tawa till it changes colour.
2. Heat 1½ tbsp oil in a non-stick pan or kadhai.
3. Add onion. Cook till soft.
4. Add broccoli, cook for 2 minutes.
5. Add paneer. Cook for 1 minute.
6. Remove pulp of tomato pieces and add to the paneer. Saute for a few seconds.
7. Remove all vegetables and paneer from the kadhai and keep aside.
8. Heat 1½ tbsp oil in a clean kadhai. Add crushed garlic and green chillies.
9. Reduce heat. Add soya sauce, tabasco or capsico sauce, chilli garlic sauce, tomato ketchup. Cook on slow fire for a few seconds.
10. Add the cooked vegetables and paneer.
11. Add salt and pepper to taste.
12. Cook for 2-3 minutes on low heat, sprinkling water occasionally, if required, till the sauces coat the paneer and vegetables.
13. Serve hot sprinkled with roasted kajus.

Step 1

Step 4, 5

Garlic Honey Paneer

Serves 3 -4

100 gms paneer- cut into 1" cubes and deep fried
a 3-4" piece of cabbage - cut into 1½" squares (1 cup)
1 small onion - cut into 4 pieces and separated
1 tbsp soya sauce
2 tsp red chilli sauce
1 tbsp tomato sauce
2 tsp honey
½ tbsp vinegar
½ tsp freshly ground pepper, ½ tsp salt, or to taste
a pinch ajinomoto (optional)
3 tbsp cornflour mixed with ¼ cup water
2-3 tbsp oil

GRIND TOGETHER
4 dry red chillies -remove seeds, break into small pieces & soak in water for 10 min
12-15 flakes garlic
1 tsp vinegar
¼ tsp jeera (cumin), 2- 3 saboot kali mirch (peppercorns)

1. Soak dry red chillies. Drain and grind to a paste with garlic, vinegar, jeera and saboot kali mirch. Keep aside.
2. Cut cabbage into 1½" square pieces. Cut onion into fours & separate the slices.
3. Dissolve cornflour in ¼ cup water and keep aside.
4. Heat oil in a kadhai. Reduce heat and add red chilli and garlic paste.
5. Stir and add onion. Mix. Add cabbage. Stir for 3-4 minutes. Add salt & pepper.
6. Stir. Reduce heat. Add chilli sauce, tomato sauce, soya sauce, honey and vinegar.
7. Add paneer and mix well for 2 minutes.
8. Pour 1½ cups of water and bring to a boil. Lower heat.
9. Add the dissolved cornflour and cook till the sauce turns thick. Serve hot.

Step 1

Step 2

Step 5

Paneer in Hot Garlic Sauce

Picture on page 97   *Serves 3-4*

150 gm cottage cheese (paneer)
2 tbsp plain flour (maida)
¼ cup cornflour
¼ tsp each of pepper & salt
¼ tsp ajinomoto (optional)
4 tbsp water

GARLIC SAUCE
15 flakes garlic or 2 tsp garlic paste
1 tbsp oil
2 tbsp tomato ketchup
1 tsp soya sauce
½ tsp white pepper, ½ tsp salt
a pinch of sugar, ¼ tsp ajinomoto (optional)
¾ cup water
1 tbsp cornflour mixed with ¼ cup water
1 spring onion greens - finely chopped (1 tbsp) for garnishing

1. To prepare the sauce, peel and grind the garlic to a rough paste.
2. Heat 1 tbsp oil and fry the garlic on low heat till it starts to change it's colour.
3. Reduce heat. Add tomato ketchup, soya sauce, pepper & salt. Cook for 1 minute.
4. Add sugar and ajinomoto.
5. Add water. Bring to a boil. Simmer for 2 minutes.
6. Add cornflour paste, stirring all the time, until the sauce thickens. Remove from heat. Keep sauce aside.
7. Cut paneer into ¾"-1" pieces.
8. Make a thick batter by mixing cornflour, plain flour, salt, pepper and ajinomoto with water.
9. Dip paneer pieces and deep fry to a golden colour.
10. At the time of serving, heat sauce. Put the fried paneer pieces and boil for 1-2 minutes till paneer turns soft. Transfer to a serving dish.
11. Garnish with spring onion greens or chopped capsicum and serve with fried rice.

Step 7

Step 9

Red Thai Curry

Serves 4-6

RED CURRY PASTE
4 Kashmiri dry, red chillies - soaked in ½ cup warm water for 10 minutes
½ onion - chopped, 8-10 flakes garlic - peeled, 1½" piece ginger - sliced
1 stalk lemon grass (use only the lower part) or rind of 1 lemon (see note)
1½ tsp coriander seeds (dhania saboot), 1 tsp cumin (jeera)
6 peppercorns (saboot kali mirch), 1 tsp salt, 1 tbsp vinegar

PANEER & VEGETABLES
200 gm paneer - cut into 1" cubes
1 small carrot - peeled and cut into fours lengthwise and then into 1" pieces
4 french beans - threaded and cut into 1" length
6-8 baby corns - cut lengthwise into 2 pieces
½ of a small broccoli or ½ of a small cauliflower - cut into medium florets (1 cup)
¼ cup chopped bamboo shoots, optional

OTHER INGREDIENTS
3 cups coconut milk, fresh or ready made (Dabur)
1 tbsp cornflour mixed in ¼ cup water
10-12 basil leaves (tulsi) or ¼ cup chopped coriander leaves
½ tsp soya sauce, salt to taste, ½ tsp brown sugar or regular sugar

1. Grind all the ingredients of the red curry paste along with the water in which the chillies were soaked, to a paste.
2. Extract 2 cups coconut milk by soaking grated coconut in 1 cup of hot water. Blend and then strain. Keep milk aside. Add more hot water to the left over coconut and blend to get 3 cups of coconut milk in all.
3. Heat 3 tbsp oil, add red curry paste. Fry for a 2 minutes on low heat.
4. Add ¼ cup of coconut milk. Add all vegetables and stir fry for 2-3 minutes.
5. Add the rest of the coconut milk, cornflour paste and soya sauce. Cover and simmer on low heat for 5-7 minutes till vegetables turn tender.
6. Add paneer, basil leaves, salt and sugar to taste. Boil for 2-3 minutes.

Note: For lemon rind, wash & grate 1 lemon with the peel gently on the grater to get lemon rind. Do not apply pressure and see that the white pith beneath the lemon peel is not grated along with the yellow rind. The white pith is bitter!

Red curry paste can be made extra & stored in an airtight box, for upto 1 month. For a bright red paste, use dry, broad big Kashmiri chillies preferably & not usual thin long ones.

Green Thai Paneer Curry
with Aubergines

Picture on page 98   *Serves 4*

200 gms paneer
2-3 small aubergines (brinjals/baingan) - peeled & cut into thin slices and sprinkled
with ¼ tsp salt
2½ cups readymade coconut milk (Dabur)
½ tsp dried basil
¾ tsp salt, 1 tsp sugar or gur
2 tbsp basil or chopped coriander leaves
2-3 green or red chillies - slit long for garnishing

GREEN CURRY PASTE
6-7 green chillies
½ onion - chopped
1 tbsp chopped garlic, ½" piece ginger - chopped
1 stick lemon grass - cut into pieces, see note
2-3 lemon leaves or ½ tsp lemon rind (see note on page 95)
4 tbsp coriander leaves, ½ tsp salt
1 tbsp white vinegar
1 tbsp coriander seeds (saboot dhania), 15 peppercorns (saboot kali mirch)
1 tbsp cumin seeds (jeera) - roasted on a tawa   *Step 1*

1. For the green curry paste, dry roast coriander seeds and cumin seeds for 2 minutes on a tawa till fragrant but not brown. Put all other ingredients of the curry paste and the roasted seeds in a grinder and grind to a fine paste, using a little water.
2. Heat oil in a kadhai. Add green curry paste. Fry for 2-3 minutes.
3. Add 1 cup coconut milk. Simmer on low heat for 5-7 minutes.
4. Add dry basil, salt, sugar, brinjals and the rest of coconut milk. Boil. Cover and cook on low heat for about 5 minutes or till brinjals are well cooked.
5. Add paneer. Give 2-3 boils.
6. Garnish with sliced red or green chillies (long thin slices), basil leaves.
7. Serve hot with boiled/steamed rice.

Note: Discard 1" from the bottom of the lemon grass. Peel a few outer leaves. Chop into ½" pieces uptil the stem. Discard the upper grass like portion.

Paneer in Hot Garlic Sauce: Recipe on page 94 ➤

Continental

◄ *Green Thai Paneer Curry with Aubergines : Recipe on page 96*

Smoky Salsa Bake

Serves 4

150 gms paneer - cut into 1" rectangular pieces of ½" thickness
200 gm big mushrooms, 1 capsicum - cut into half from the middle, some butter

SALSA
5 tomatoes - roasted, 1 tbsp oil
2 onions - chopped finely, 1 green chilli - chopped
2 tbsp chopped coriander, 1 tbsp cornflour
1 tbsp tomato ketchup, 2 tsp vinegar
1 tsp salt and ¼ tsp pepper, or to taste

MIX TOGETHER
½ tsp freshly crushed pepper, 1 tsp oregano, ½ cup grated cheese (mozzarella)

1. To prepare salsa, pierce a tomato with a fork. Hold it over the naked flame to roast it till the skin turns blackish and charred. Roast all the tomatoes like this.
2. Cool the tomatoes and peel. Chop 2 tomatoes and puree the other 3 tomatoes.
3. Heat oil and saute onion and green chillies till onion turns soft. Add all other ingredients and cook for 2-3 minutes. Remove the salsa from fire.
4. Wash capsicum and mushrooms. Pat dry on a clean cloth. Rub melted butter on them all over. Insert a fork or a knife on to the greased capsicum. Roast on a naked flame, turning sides, directly on the heat till charred (slightly blackened) from various sides. Roast for 2-3 minutes. Cool. Cut the smoked capsicum into slices widthwise to get half rings. Roast the mushrooms also in the same way on a naked flame and cut each lengthwise into 3-4 thick slices.
5. Roast paneer without butter on the naked flame in the same way with forks. To hasten the process you can use 4 forks on the same flame at the same time.
6. Spread the salsa in an oven proof dish. Arrange mushrooms to cover completely.
7. Sprinkle cheese mixed with pepper and oregano.
8. Spread the roasted capsicum and the paneer. Sprinkle salt and pepper.
9. To serve, heat in an oven or a microwave. Serve.

Step 1

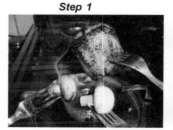

Step 7

Step 8

Baked Corn with Paneer

Paneer is marinated in mustard dressing and then baked with corn in a mustard sauce.

Serves 2-3

200 gm cottage cheese (paneer) - cut into thin, 1" pieces
½ cup green capsicum
1 cup tinned corn kernels
30 whole, small spinach leaves - remove stem and tear each leaf into half
6 tbsp grated cheese, preferably mozzarella cheese
3 tbsp chopped walnuts (akhrot)

MARINADE
1 tsp mustard paste
1 tsp lemon juice
¼ tsp freshly ground peppercorns (saboot kali mirch), ½ tsp salt

MUSTARD SAUCE
2 tbsp butter
1 small onion - chopped finely, 2 tbsp maida (plain flour)
2 cups milk, 1 tsp salt, ¾ tsp pepper
½ tsp dried basil or 2 tbsp fresh basil leaves or tender leaves of tulsi
2 tsp mustard paste

1. Cut the paneer into 1" pieces of ¼" thickness. Marinate them with mustard paste, lemon juice, salt and pepper. Mix well. Keep aside.

Step 1

2. To make the mustard sauce, melt butter in a kadhai or pan. Add onions and stir till soft. Add flour and stir on low heat for a minute.
3. Add capsicum and corn. Stir for ½ minute.
4. Add milk, stirring continuously and cook till it coats the back of a spoon.
5. Add basil, salt, pepper and mustard paste. Remove from fire. Keep sauce aside.

Step 9

6. Arrange spinach leaves overlapping slightly in a small, greased borosil dish.
7. Arrange the paneer over the spinach leaves.
8. Pour the prepared mustard sauce over it.
9. Arrange spinach overlapping slightly on the sauce.
10. Mix grated cheese and walnuts and sprinkle on top. Bake at 180°C for 15 minutes till cheese melts.

Cottage Cheese Florentine

The word florentine is associated with spinach. Here we have a quick and tasty recipe of paneer flavoured with fennel on a bed of shredded spinach, topped with mushroom sauce.

Serves 3-4

200-250 gm paneer - cut into 1½" square pieces of ½" thickness

MARINADE
1 tsp saunf (fennel) - roughly crushed, 1 tsp Worcestershire sauce
½ tbsp butter, ¼ tsp salt

SPINACH BED
1 tbsp butter, 3-4 flakes garlic - crushed & chopped (1 tsp)
250 gm spinach - shredded (2½ cups)
salt and pepper to taste

MUSHROOM SAUCE
1 tbsp butter, salt and pepper to taste
150 gm mushrooms - chopped finely, 1 tsp Worcestershire sauce
1 tsp cornflour dissolved in ½ cup water

TOPPING
50 gm cheese (mozzarella or cheddar) - grated (½ cup)

1. Marinate the paneer with fennel, 1 tsp of Worcestershire sauce and a little salt. Keep the paneer aside.

Step 1

2. To cook spinach, heat 1 tbsp of butter in a non stick pan on low heat. As soon as the butter melts, add garlic. Stir and add the spinach. Stir fry spinach mashing well, till all the water evaporates. Add a little salt and freshly ground pepper. Transfer spinach to a serving dish.

3. In the same pan add ½ tbsp butter and saute the marinated paneer pieces till light brown on both sides. Arrange pan fried paneer on the cooked spinach.

Step 6

4. For the sauce, heat 1 tbsp of butter in a clean pan. Add the mushrooms and stir till light brown.

5. Add 1 tsp Worcestershire sauce, salt and pepper to taste.

6. Pour in the dissolved cornflour paste and stir till slightly thick. Remove sauce from fire and pour the sauce over the cottage cheese.

7. Top with grated cheese. Grill in an oven or a microwave for 2-3 minutes till cheese melts.

Cubed Paneer & Veg Sizzler

Serves 2

100 gms paneer - cut into ½" cubes
6 mushrooms - cut into halves
1 small onion - cut into 4 pieces and separated
1 carrot - cut into small cubes and boiled
½ capsicum - cut into ½" pieces
1 slice of tinned pineapple - cut into small pieces
½ tsp salt and ½ tsp freshly crushed pepper, or to taste

SAUCE
6-7 flakes garlic - crushed, 2 tbsp oil
2 green chillies - deseeded & chopped finely
½ tbsp soya sauce, a few drops tabasco or capsico sauce
1 tbsp red chilli sauce, 3 tbsp tomato ketchup
1 tbsp vinegar, ¼ tsp pepper and ½ tsp salt, or to taste
2 level tbsp cornflour dissolved in 1½ cups water

TO SERVE
2 tbsp butter
a sizzler plate, rice boiled with salt and lemon juice

1. Heat 2 tbsp oil in a non-stick pan or kadhai. Add mushrooms. Saute till light brown and dry. Add onion. Saute for 2 minutes. Add carrots. Stir for 1-2 minutes.
2. Add capsicum, pineapple and paneer. Add salt and freshly crushed pepper. Cook for 1 minute. Remove all vegetables and paneer from the kadhai and keep aside.
3. To prepare the sauce, heat 2 tbsp oil in a clean kadhai. Reduce heat. Add garlic & green chillies. Stir for a few seconds on low heat till garlic just changes colour.
4. Remove from fire. Add all sauces and vinegar. Cook on slow fire for a few seconds. Add salt and pepper to taste. Add cornflour paste, stirring continuously till a sauce is ready. Add vegetables and paneer. Cook for 1 minute on low heat.
5. To serve, remove the iron sizzler plate from the wooden base. Heat the iron plate by keeping it directly on the flame. Reduce heat and let the iron plate be on fire while it is being filled. Put 2-3 tbsp water in the wooden base and scatter 1 tbsp butter cut into pieces on the wooden base. Keep wooden base aside.
6. When the iron plate is heated, scatter 1 tbsp butter here and there. Place 2-3 cabbage leaves on the plate and arrange rice on it. Leave on slow flame for 2 minutes for the rice to get heated. Put the hot vegetables in sauce in the centre portion of the rice. When the hot sauce falls on the hot plate, it sizzles. With the help of a firm pair of tongs (sansi), place the iron plate on the wooden tray. Serve sizzling hot.

Stuffed Cheese Steaks

Picture on page 108   *Serves 4*

400 gm paneer - cut into 1½"x 2" squares of 1" thickness

FILLING
6-7 french beans - cut into paper thin slices
¼ cup finely grated carrot (½ carrot)
¼ tsp salt, ¼ tsp oregano, a pinch of pepper, or to taste
½ cube cheese - grated finely (2 tbsp)
½ tbsp butter, 1 tbsp grated onion (½ onion)

PEPPER SAUCE
2 tsp chopped garlic, ½ tsp ginger paste
½ tsp peppercorns (saboot kali mirch) - crushed, 4 peppercorns (saboot kali mirch)
½-1 tsp soya sauce, 1 tbsp tomato ketchup, a pinch of ajinomoto, 1 tsp vinegar
1½ tbsp cornflour, 2 tbsp butter or oil
1½ cups hot water mixed with 1 vegetable-seasoning cube (Maggi)

BATTER
3 tbsp plain flour (maida), ¼ cup plus 1 tbsp milk
2 pinches haldi, ¼ tsp salt, ¼ tsp red chilli powder, 2 tbsp very finely grated cheese

1. Cut paneer into thick, big rectangular pieces. Divide each piece into 2 pieces. Sprinkle salt & freshly ground pepper on both sides on each piece and keep aside.
2. For the filling, heat butter. Add onion. Stir fry for 2 minutes. Add beans. Cook covered for 3 minutes on low heat till soft. Add carrots, salt, pepper, oregano, grated cheese and stir for 1 minute. Remove from fire and keep aside to cool.
3. Take a piece of paneer. Spread 1 tsp of the filling on it. Press another piece of paneer on it. Turn and press the other side also to join properly. Keep aside.
4. For the batter, mix all ingredients of the batter together. Keep aside.
5. For pepper sauce, mix cornflour in ½ cup water. Keep aside the cornflour paste.
6. Heat butter, reduce heat & add garlic, ginger paste, crushed peppercorns & whole peppercorns. Cook till garlic changes colour. Add soya sauce, tomato ketchup, ajinomoto & vinegar. Add hot water mixed with seasoning cube. Boil.
7. Add cornflour paste. Cook stirring continuously till sauce thickens slightly. Remove from fire. Do not overcook the sauce; otherwise it gets very thick.
8. At serving time heat ½ tbsp butter in a nonstick pan on medium heat. Dip the stuffed steak in the prepared batter to coat all sides and put in the pan. Cook 4 pieces at a time. Reduce heat after 2 minutes when the edges start changing colour. Turn the side gently with a flat spoon. Cook till browned on both sides.
9. Top steaks with some pepper sauce and serve the remaining sauce separately.

Broccoli & Paneer in

Lemon Cream Sauce

Serves 3- 4

100 gm paneer - cut into ½" cubes
1 small flower of broccoli - cut into ½" florets (100 gms) with very little stalks
¼ cup broccoli crumbs (grate a small piece of broccoli to get crumbs)
1 small onion- sliced
1½ tbsp butter, 1½ tbsp olive oil or any cooking oil
2-3 flakes garlic - minced or very finely chopped
¼ tsp ajwain (carom seeds)

MIXTURE
1½ tbsp lemon juice, 1 tsp tomato ketchup
½ cup cream, ¼ cup milk
2 tbsp finely sliced chives or spring onion greens or chopped parsley
½ tsp salt and ½ tsp freshly ground pepper, or to taste
1 tsp cornflour, ½ cup water

1. Mix all ingredients together given under mixture in a bowl and keep aside.
2. Heat the butter and oil in a pan.
3. Add ajwain and garlic and cook for 1 minute.
4. Add the sliced onion and cook till soft.
5. Add broccoli crumbs, cook for a minute.
6. Add broccoli florets and cook for 2-3 minutes. Add ¼ tsp salt and ¼ tsp pepper.
7. Add the mixed ingredients in the bowl to the broccoli in the pan. Mix well.

Step 7

8. Reduce heat, add paneer and bring to a boil, stirring constantly. Cook for 1 minute until a sauce is ready. Remove from fire.
9. Serve hot with garlic bread cut into slices, drizzled with olive oil and made crisp golden in the oven.

Iman Binaldey

Picture on facing page   *Serves 6*

100 gm cottage cheese (paneer) - cut into very tiny cubes
2 cups kabuli channa (chick peas) - soaked overnight, a pinch of mitha soda
¼ of red, yellow or green capsicum, for garnish

WHITE SAUCE

2½ tbsp butter, 1 onion - finely chopped, 2½ tbsp plain flour (maida), 2 cups milk
1 tsp salt and ¼ tsp pepper, or to taste, ½ cup grated cheddar cheese (tin or cubes)

TOMATO SAUCE

1 onion - cut into thin slices, ½ kg tomatoes - blended to a puree in a mixer
3 tbsp readymade tomato puree, 2 tbsp tomato sauce
4 flakes garlic - crushed, ¼ cup basil or coriander leaves
1 tsp dried oregano, ½ tsp chilli powder, ½ tsp sugar, 1 tsp salt, or to taste

1. To boil channas, drain the water from the channas. Add 4 cups water, 1½ tsp salt and a pinch of mitha soda. Pressure cook to give one whistle. Keep on low heat for about 10 minutes. Remove from fire. Keep aside.

2. To prepare the white sauce, melt the butter in a heavy bottomed pan or a kadhai. Add onion and stir till it just changes colour. Sprinkle flour and cook on low heat for 1 minute without browning, stirring throughout. Remove from heat and gradually add the milk. Mix until well blended. Return to heat and cook slowly for about 2 minutes on low heat, stirring throughout until the sauce thickens and coats the spoon well. Remove from fire. Add cheese, salt and pepper. Mix well.

3. For the tomato sauce, heat 2 tbsp oil and fry the onion for 2-3 minutes till it slightly changes colour. Add the fresh tomato puree, ready made tomato puree, tomato sauce, garlic and basil leaves. Add 1 tsp oregano, ½ tsp chilli powder, ½ tsp sugar and 1 tsp salt. Boil for 10 minutes on low heat till the juice from the tomatoes evaporates and it turns slightly thick. Add the boiled channas along with the water. Cook till the extra water evaporates and the tomato masala coats the channas slightly. Add paneer. Mix. Check salt etc. and remove from fire.

4. In a borosil dish, spread 4 tbsp white sauce at the base.

5. Spread channas on white sauce, filling the dish.

6. Spread the remaining white sauce with a tbsp on channas, leaving gaps of 2" in between. This way you get red & white strips. Start from the corner, dropping a few tbsp of white sauce in a row, leave a gap & then drop some white sauce in a row. This way you get a red and white striped look.

Step 6

7. Arrange a few coloured capsicum slices diagonally on the white row. Bake in a preheated oven for 20 minutes at 200° C. Serve hot.

Noodles
Rice & Rotis

◄ *Stuffed Paneer Steaks: Recipe on page 104*

Dum Hyderabadi Biryani

Picture on page 127   *Serves 6*

RICE
2 cups (250 gm) basmati rice - washed and kept in the strainer for 30 minutes
4-5 chhoti illaichi (green cardamom)
2 tej patta (bay leaves), 5-6 laung (cloves)
3 tsp salt, 1 tbsp lemon juice, 10 cups water

VEGETABLES
2 thin carrots - peeled and cut into round slices
20 french beans - cut into ¼" pieces
½ of a small cauliflower - cut into small florets

MIX TOGETHER
1½ cups curd
1 tbsp mint - chopped finely, 1 tbsp coriander - chopped finely
2-3 drops kewra essence or ½ tsp ruh kewra, ½ tsp salt

CRUSHED SPICES TOGETHER
½ tsp shah jeera (black cumin), 3-4 blades javetri (mace)
seeds of 1 moti illaichi, 1 stick of dalchini (cinnamon)

OTHER INGREDIENTS
4-5 tbsp melted ghee or oil
50 gms paneer - cut into tiny square pieces for topping
8-10 almonds - split into two pieces, 1 tbsp kishmish (raisins)
2 large onion - sliced, 3 tsp ginger-garlic paste
1 tsp red chilli powder, 1½ tsp salt
a few mint leaves (poodina)
orange and yellow colour
seeds of 4 chhoti illaichi - crushed to a powder, 1 tbsp melted ghee

TO SEAL
aluminium foil and dough

1. Wash rice several times. Strain. Let it be in the strainer for 30 minutes. (Do not soak).
2. Boil 10 cups water with all ingredients given under rice - chhoti illaichi, laung, tej patta, salt and lemon juice.
3. When the water boils, throw in the rice. Stir. Boil just for 4-5 minutes so that the rice is a little chewy and not fully soft.
4. Remove from fire. If you find the grains too hard, let them be in hot water for 2 minutes. Strain in a big steel strainer or a colander. Run a fork frequently in the

Contd...

rice to separate the grains of rice. Let the rice be in the strainer for 10 minutes to drain out all the water. Now spread rice in a big tray on a cloth. Keep under the fan for 10 minutes. Remove whole spices from the cooked rice & discard them.

5. Heat ghee or oil. Add almonds and kishmish and paneer. Stir for a few seconds. Remove from oil and keep aside for topping.

6. Add onions & stir till rich brown. Remove half onion & keep aside for garnish. Reduce heat. Add crushed spices, ginger-garlic paste, chilli powder & salt. Mix.

7. Add vegetables and stir for 2 minutes.

8. Reduce heat. Add ½ of the curd mixture leaving some to put on rice later on.

9. Stir to mix. Cook, stirring on low heat till the vegetables are just done or crisp-tender. Do not over cook. After the vegetables are done, a little masala, about ¼ cup should remain (semi dry). If the vegetables turn too dry, add ¼ cup water. Boil. Remove from fire.

Step 10

10. To assemble the biryani, take a handi or a baking dish. Grease it. Spread 1/3 of the rice in the dish. Spoon some curd on the rice.
Sprinkle yellow colour on half of the rice and orange colour on the other half of the rice.

11. Spread half of the vegetables over the rice.

12. Put ½ the rice on the vegetables. Spoon ½ of the curd mix on the rice. Sprinkle colours. Do not mix.

Step 12

13. Repeat vegetable layer using all the vegetable.

14. Spread remaining rice. Spoon curd on it. Sprinkle colours. Do not mix.

15. Sprinkle illaichi powder and 1 tbsp of melted ghee over the rice. Put a few mint leaves on the rice.

16. Sprinkle browned onions, fried paneer, almonds and kishmish. Cover with foil.

17. Take a big ball of atta dough, roll in into a long strip.

18. Cover the handi with a foil nicely, pressing the edges well. Seal the end of the handi by pressing the dough strip on the foil, sticking it with the handi.

19. Keep in the oven, if using a glass dish, for 'dum' at 150°C for 30 minutes or keep on a tawa, if using a metal handi, on very low heat for 15-20 minutes.

Step 17

Step 18

Chinese Fried Rice

Serves 4

1½ cups uncooked rice, preferably golden Sela rice (parboiled rice)
¼ cup very finely sliced French beans
1 carrot - finely diced (cut into tiny cubes)
2 spring onions - chopped along with the greens
2 green chillies - chopped finely
2 flakes garlic - chopped & crushed
½ of a big capsicum - diced
2 tbsp oil
½ tsp of each of pepper & ajinomoto
1 tsp soya sauce (according to the colour desired)
1 tsp vinegar, optional
1 tsp salt or to taste

1. Clean, wash and soak rice for 10 minutes. Boil 6 cups water with 2 tsp salt. Drain and add rice to boiling water. Cook uncovered till the rice is just done and still firm. Do not overcook. Strain. Keep in the strainer for 10 minutes to let all the water drain out. Fluff up the rice with a fork to let the steam escape and to separate the grains of rice. Spread out the cooked rice on a large tray and keep under the fan to dry out nicely. (This makes it turn a little chewy, as the Chinese like it.)
2. Chop green and white part of spring onions separately.
3. Heat oil in large kadhai or pan. Reduce heat. Add green chillies. Add garlic and white of onions.
4. Add beans, then carrots. Stir fry for 1 minute. Add capsicum.
5. Add salt, pepper and ajinomoto. Add rice. Add soya sauce and vinegar.
6. Add the green onions & salt to taste. Stir fry the rice for 2-3 minutes. Serve hot.

Haka Noodles

CHILLI NOODLES
400 gms haka noodles - boiled & spread in a tray
4 tbsp oil
4-5 dry, whole red chillies - broken into bits
½ tsp chilli flakes or powder
2 tsp salt
1 tsp Soya sauce

OTHER INGREDIENTS
1 capsicum - cut into thin long pieces
1 carrot - cut into fine juliennes or match sticks
1 cup shredded cabbage
6-8 flakes garlic - crushed and chopped, optional
2 spring onions or 1 small onion - shredded
2 tbsp bean sprouts - optional
1 tbsp dried black mushrooms or 3- 4 fresh mushrooms - finely sliced
1 tbsp vinegar
½ tsp ajinomoto
1 tsp salt, ½ tsp pepper

1. To boil noodles, in a large pan boil 12 cups water with 2 tsp salt and 1 tbsp oil. Add noodles to the boiling water. Cook uncovered on high flame for about 2-3 minutes only. Drain. Wash in cold water several times. Strain. Leave in the strainer for 15-20 minutes, turning them upside down, once after about 10 minutes to ensure complete drying. Apply 1 tbsp oil on the noodles and keep aside for 30 minutes.

2. Heat 4-5 tbsp oil. Remove from fire; add broken red chillies and red chilli flakes or powder.

3. Return to fire and mix in the boiled noodles, using two forks. Add salt and a little Soya sauce. Do not add too much Soya sauce. Fry for 2-3 minutes, till the noodles turn a pale brown. Keep the fried noodles aside.

4. Heat 2 tbsp oil. Reduce heat and add garlic. Cook for ½ minute.

5. Add vegetables in sequence of their tenderness - onions, sprouts, mushrooms, capsicum, carrot and cabbage. Add vinegar.

6. Add ajinomoto, salt and pepper. Cook for ½ minute.

7. Slide in the noodles and mix well using 2 forks. Serve hot.

Masaman Thai Rice

Delicious aromatic rice which can be had plain without any side dish. A complete meal in itself. Almost like a vegetarian masala biryani.

Serves 3-4

1 cup basmati rice - soaked for 10-15 minutes
50 gms paneer - diced to get small squares (½ cup)
1 carrot - diced, 1 small capsicum - diced
2½ tsp salt, ½ tsp haldi powder
2 stalks lemon grass - tie into a knot, see note
3½ tbsp lemon juice, 4 tbsp oil
one packet coconut powder (maggi) mixed with 1½ cups water and 1 cup milk
or 2½ cups coconut milk

MASAMAN PASTE (makes ½ cup apporx.)
5 dried, red chillies - deseed and soak in water for 15-20 minutes
6 tbsp chopped onions or shallots, 6-7 large flakes garlic, 2 tsp chopped ginger
3 sticks lemon grass - the lower stem is cut into small pieces, discard the leaves
1 tbsp cumin seeds (jeera), 1 tsp saunf (fennel)
1" stick cinnamon (dalchini), seeds of 2 moti illaichi (brown cardamom)
¼ tsp grated jaiphal (nutmeg), 1 tbsp coriander seeds (saboot dhania)
2 cloves (laung), 4 black peppercorns (saboot kali mirch)

1. For paste, roast all ingredients of the masaman paste on a tawa/ kadhai/wok for 5 minutes or till fragrant.
2. Grind to a fine paste. Use little water if needed.
3. Mix one packet coconut milk powder (maggi) with 1½ cups of water and 1 cup milk. Keep coconut milk aside.
4. Heat 4 tbsp oil in a pan with a well fitted lid. Add the prepared masaman curry paste. Fry till aromatic and leaves oil.
5. Reduce heat, add ½ cup of prepared coconut milk. Cook till nearly dry.
6. Add carrot. Stir fry for a minute.
7. Add salt, haldi, lemon juice, lemon grass, remaining coconut milk, paneer, capsicum and the soaked rice. Give one boil.
8. Cook covered for 8-10 minutes or till all the water has dried and the rice is cooked. Discard lemon grass.
9. Serve hot garnished with lemon wedges and tomato slices.

Note: The lower stem of lemon grass is used for the paste and the upper grass is tied into a knot and used for flavouring rice, soups etc and then discarded later. If lemon grass is not available for paste use rind of 2 whole lemons.

Tandoori Paneer Parantha

Serves 4

2 cups (250 gms) atta (whole wheat flour)
1 cup (200 ml) water - approx.
½ tsp salt
2-3 tbsp solid ghee
kasoori methi (dry fenugreek leaves)

FILLING
100 gms paneer - mashed
1 onion - chopped finely
1 green chilli - chopped finely
¾ tsp salt
¾ tsp red chilli powder
¾ tsp garam masala

1. Keep ghee in the fridge for some time, so that it solidifies.
2. Make a soft dough with atta, salt and water. Keep aside for ½ hour.
3. Mix all ingredients of the filling. Keep aside.
4. Divide the dough into 6 equal parts. Shape into round balls.
5. Flatten each ball, roll out each into a round of 5" diameter.
6. Spread 1 tsp full of solidified ghee. Then spread 1 tbsp of filling all over.
7. Make a slit, starting from the centre till any one end.
8. Start rolling from the slit, to form an even cone.
9. Keeping the cone upright, press slightly.
10. Roll out, applying pressure only at the centre. Do not roll or press two much on the sides, otherwise the layers of parantha do not separate after cooking.
11. Sprinkle some kasoori methi and press with a rolling pin (belan).
12. Apply water on the back side of the parantha and stick carefully in a heated tandoor or place in a preheated oven in a greased tray.
13. Remove after a few minutes.
14. Spread some ghee, serve hot.

Step 7

Step 8

Step 9

Tandoori Platter with BBQ Sauce

Picture on facing page   *Serves 8*

250 gm paneer - cut into large (1½") cubes, 2 capsicums - cut into large cubes
200 gm (10-12) mushrooms - trim ends of the stalks, leaving them whole
100 gm baby corns - blanched with a pinch of haldi & 1 tsp salt in 3 cups water
8 cherry tomatoes or 1 large tomato - cut into 8 pieces & pulp removed
1 onion - cut into fours & separated

MARINADE
1 cup thick curd - hang for 30 minutes in a muslin cloth
2 tbsp thick cream
2 tbsp oil
1 tbsp cornflour
1 tbsp thick ginger-garlic paste
½ tsp black salt (kala namak)
¼ tsp haldi or tandoori colour
2 tsp tandoori masala
½ tsp red chilli powder
¾ tsp salt or to taste

BARBECUE SAUCE
3 tbsp butter or oil
4-5 flakes garlic - crushed
2 large tomatoes - pureed till smooth
¼ cup ready made tomato puree
¼ tsp red chilli powder, ½ tsp pepper, ¾ tsp salt or to taste
¼ tsp sugar
½ tsp worcestershire sauce
½ tsp soya sauce

RICE
1 cup uncooked rice - soaked for 1 hour
1 tbsp sugar
2 tbsp oil
½ tsp jeera (cumin seeds)
2 small onions - sliced finely
1" stick dalchini (cinnamon)
2 tej patta (bay leaves), 2 laung (cloves)
2 chhoti illaichi (green cardamoms)
3-4 saboot kali mirch (peppercorns)
1 tsp salt or to taste

Contd...

1. For the marinade, hang curd in a muslin cloth for ½ hour.

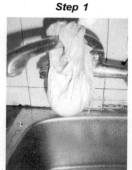

2. For rice, mix sugar with 3 tbsp water in a small heavy bottomed vessel. Cook on low flame till it is rich brown in colour. Add two cups of hot water to it. Stir till dissolved. Remove from fire and keep aside.

3. Heat oil. Add jeera. When it turns golden add onions and stir fry till golden brown in colour. Add all whole masalas.

4. Add the rice. Fry for a while. Add caramel sugar water and salt. Cover and cook on a very low fire till the water gets absorbed and the rice is done. Keep aside.

5. For vegetables, rub oil generously on a wire rack or grill of the oven.

6. Mix all ingredients of the marinade. Add paneer, mushrooms and baby corns to the marinade and mix well to coat the marinade. Remove from bowl and arrange on the rack or on greased wooden skewers. In the remaining marinade which is sticking to the sides of the bowl, add onion, capsicum and tomatoes. Leave these in the bowl itself. Marinate all for atleast ½ hour.

7. Grill paneer and vegetables in the oven at 210°C/410°F for 12-15 minutes or roast in a gas tandoor, on the wire rack or on skewers. Spoon a little oil/melted butter (basting) on them. Add onion, capsicum and tomatoes. Grill for another 5-7 minutes.

8. For the sauce, heat oil in a kadhai. Add garlic and cook till light brown.

9. Add fresh tomato puree, ready made tomato puree and chilli powder. Cook for 5 minutes till well blended. Add all other ingredients and ½ cup water to get a thin sauce. Boil. Simmer for 2 minutes. Remove from fire and keep aside.

10. To serve, heat rice separately in a microwave or an oven. Spread the rice on a serving plate. Put some hot sauce on the rice. Arrange grilled. Pour some hot sauce over the vegetables. Serve the extra sauce in a separate sauce boat or bowl. Serve at once.

◄ **Kiwi Cheese Cake: Recipe on page 126**

The Sweet Touch

Chenna Kulfi

The khoya is substituted with low fat paneer.

Serves 15

1 kg (5 cups) milk - at room temperature
½ cup sugar
75 gm paneer - grated finely (¾ cup)
2 tbsp cornflour
seeds of 3-4 chhoti illaichi (green cardamoms) - crushed
1 tbsp kishmish (raisins)
1 tbsp shredded badam (almonds)

1. Dissolve cornflour in ¼ cup milk.
2. Heat the rest of the milk with sugar. Boil and keep on fire for about 20 minutes, till reduced to half the quantity.
3. Add illaichi.
4. Add the cornflour paste to the boiling milk, stirring continuously.
5. Continue boiling, by lowering the flame, for about 2-3 minutes. Cool.
6. Add paneer, kishmish and almonds. Check sugar. Remove from fire.
7. Fill in clean kulfi moulds and leave to set in the freezer for 6-8 hours.

Step 7

Stuffed Khubani in Syrup

Serves 8-10   *Picture on page 1*

**13 large dried imported seedless khubani (dried apricots, orange in colour)
some rose petals and chhoti illaichi (green cardamom), to garnish**

FILLING
**50 gms paneer - grated very finely
seeds of 3 chhoti illaichi - powdered
5-6 badaam (almonds) - crushed coarsely, a drop of kewra essence**

SYRUP
**½ cup of sugar, 1 cup of water, 2-3 chhoti illaichi (green cardamoms)
2 drops of kewra essence**

Step 1

1. Take a khubani, make a small slit at one side of the khubani.
2. Insert the knife straight inside without puncturing at any side. Rotate the knife gently, creating space for filling. Let the other end be intact. Do not puncture it, otherwise the filling will come out.

Step 2

3. For filling, grate paneer very finely. Add powdered illaichi seeds, crushed badaam and kewra essence. Mix gently.
4. For the syrup, heat sugar, water and illaichi together in a pan. Give 2- 3 boils. Cook on low heat for 3-4 minutes. Add essence.
5. Add khubani to the syrup and let it cook for another 2-3 minutes. Remove from fire. Let it cool in the syrup.
6. Take one piece of khubani at a time. Fill atleast ½- 1 tsp of filling in each piece. Keep pushing the filling inside, to get more space for filling more. Push gently.
7. Put back in the syrup. Keep in the fridge for atleast 2-3 hours before serving for the dessert to taste good.
8. At serving time, garnish with rose petals and illaichi. Serve at room temperature.

Step 6

Step 7

Shahi Paneer Kheer with Lychees

A very decorative & a delicious dessert with an Indian flavour. Assure your guests that the seed of the lychee has been removed and replaced with a blanched almond to enjoy the fruit comfortably. When lychees are not available, make balls with a small scooper of any fruit available.

Picture on page 87   *Serves 8-10*

20-25 large lychees
20-25 almonds - blanched (soaked in hot water and skin removed)
10 sheets of varq (silver sheets)
½ tin of milk maid (condensed milk) (¾ cup)
½ cup of milk
250 gm paneer - grated
¼ tsp kesar (saffron) - soaked in 1 tbsp rose water
300 gm cream - chilled nicely and whipped till it turns thick

GARNISH
a few rose petals
a few green pistas - sliced

1. Peel and carefully deseed the lychees, keeping the lychees whole.
2. Insert one almond in each lychee in place of the seed.
3. Open up a varq carefully. Place 2 lychees with the broad end (open end) downwards on the sheet leaving some space in-between the two lychees. Carefully lift the paper beneath the varq to coat the lychees with varq. Do not touch the varq directly. Keep the pearly lychees covered in a plate and refrigerate.
4. Soak the saffron in rose water.
5. Whip the chilled cream (chill the cream before whipping) till slightly thick.
6. Beat ½ tin condensed milk, ½ cup milk and saffron along with the rose water in a pan till smooth.
7. Add the grated paneer and mix well.
8. Add cream to the condensed milk mixture to get a kheer like consistency of the mixture (thick pouring consistency). If you like it less sweet, add some more grated paneer.
9. Transfer to a shallow serving dish. Top the milk maid mixture with pearly lychees. Garnish with rose petals and sliced pistas. Serve chilled.

Bread and Paneer Pudding

A very decorative & a delicious Indian bread pudding.

Serves 8-10

6 slices of bread - sides removed and each cut into 4 pieces and deep fried till golden brown
5 tbsp of chopped mixed nuts (badam, kishmish, pista etc.)
¼ cup cold milk

PANEER LAYER
4 cups milk, ½ cup sugar, ¾ tsp powdered chhoti illaichi
8 tsp cornflour dissolved in ½ cup milk
100 gms paneer (cottage cheese) - grated
2 drops of kewra essence

1. For the paneer layer, boil 4 cups milk. Simmer on low flame for 20 minutes.
2. In the meanwhile, boil sugar with ½ cup water in a separate pan. Keep on low heat for 5 minutes. Add grated paneer. Cook for 1 minute. Remove from fire.
3. Add cornflour paste to the milk of step 1, stirring continuously. Keep stirring for 2 minutes till thick.
4. Add the prepared sugar & paneer mixture. Boil. Keep on heat for 1 minute. Remove from fire. Cool.
5. Add essence. Sprinkle illaichi powder. Keep aside.
6. Remove the side crusts of bread. Heat oil in a kadhai. Deep fry each piece till golden brown. Let it cool.
7. Dip each piece of bread in some cold milk for a second. Remove immediately. Cut each slice into 4 square pieces. This way you get 24 small pieces of bread.
8. Take a serving dish. Spread 1 tbsp of paneer layer at the bottom of the dish. Place pieces of fried bread together in a single layer to cover the base of the dish.
9. Spread about ½ tsp of the paneer mixture on each piece. Sprinkle 1 tbsp of chopped mixed nuts on the paneer.
10. Repeat the bread layer in the same way with bread pieces first then the paneer layer and finally topped with 1½ tbsp of chopped mixed nuts.
11. Repeat with the left over bread, paneer and nuts to get a 3 layered pudding. Cover with a cling wrap (plastic film) and let it set for atleast ½ hour before serving. Serve at room temperature.

Step 1

Step 2

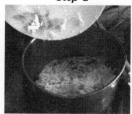

Step 10

Pina Cheese Cake

A delicious cheese cake which is made without cream. A guilt free dessert. The green coloured swirls on top makes it an eye pleasing dessert.

Picture on page 2　　　　　　　　*Serves 8-10*

BASE
25 marie biscuits
8 tbsp milk
2½ tbsp melted butter

CHEESE CAKE FILLING
2 cups grated paneer
2-3 tbsp cheese spread (plain)
2 cups curd (yogurt) - hang in a muslin cloth for 20-30 minutes
1 tin pineapple (small), see note
4 tsp gelatine
9 tbsp powdered sugar
2 egg whites, optional
½ tsp pineapple essence
few drops of yellow colour
rind of 1 lemon
1 tbsp lemon juice

TOPPING
1 tsp cornflour
1 tsp sugar
½ cup milk
½ tsp pineapple or lemon essence, few drops green colour
a lemon twist
1-2 pineapple slices

1. Crush biscuits roughly. Place the biscuits in a small mixer grinder and add 8 tbsp milk and 2½ tbsp melted butter. Blend till smooth and slightly moist.

2. Press the biscuits at the bottom of a loose bottom tin of 8" diameter or a glass serving dish. Level it with the back of steel bowl (katori). Place in the fridge to set.

Step 2

3. Place hung curd (measure to 1 cup), paneer and cheese spread in a blender and blend to a very smooth paste. Check with the fingers to see that it is no longer grainy. Remove to a bowl.

4. Separate the pineapple syrup from the pineapple rings.
5. Take 1 cup pineapple syrup (from the tin) in a pan. Add ½ cup water to it. Sprinkle gelatine on this syrup for 2-3 minutes and gently heat (do not bring to boil) till gelatine dissolves. Remove from fire.

Step 7

6. Add the hot gelatine solution gradually, stirring continuously with the other hand, to the yogurt mixture. Mix well. Add sugar. Keep aside.
7. For lemon rind, wash & grate 1 firm lemon with the peel gently on the grater to get lemon rind. Do not apply pressure and see that the white pith beneath the lemon peel is not grated along with the yellow rind. The white pith is bitter!
8. Add the essence, lemon juice, rind and colour also to the cheese cake mixture. Mix well.
9. Place in the freezer compartment for 10-15 minutes or till slightly thick.
10. Chop 4 pieces pineapple into tiny pieces.
11. Beat the egg whites till stiff, if using.
12. Remove the cheese cake mix from the freezer and beat with a spoon.

Step 11

13. Fold in stiff egg whites & pineapple pieces gently.
14. Pour over the biscuit base. Keep in the fridge to set.
15. For the topping, mix cornflour and sugar in milk and keep on fire. Bring to a boil, stirring continuously, till a thick sauce is ready. Remove from fire and let it cool down. Add colour and essence.

Step 14

16. Pour in circles on the set cheese cake with a spoon. Arrange pineapple pieces on the sides. Cut a slice from a lemon. Cut it from any one end till the centre and then twist it gently. Arrange the lemon twist in the centre. Serve cold.

Note: Store the leftover pineapple rings in a steel or plastic box in the freezer compartment of the refrigerator for 2-3 months without getting spoilt.

Kiwi Cheese Cake

Picture on page 118   Serves 12

BASE
20 marie biscuits, 6 tbsp milk, 2 tbsp melted butter

CHEESE CAKE FILLING
2 kiwis - peeled and ground to a puree, 4 tbsp sugar
2 cups curd (yogurt) - hang in a muslin cloth for 20-30 minutes
2 cups finely grated paneer (200 gm)
2 tbsp cheese spread (plain), 7 tbsp powdered sugar
4 tsp gelatine, few drops of green colour, 2 egg whites, optional

TOPPING
1 kiwi - blend to a puree with ¼ cup water
2 tsp gelatine - soaked in ½ cup water, 3 tbsp sugar, a few drops green colour

DECORATIVE ICING (OPTIONAL)
75 gms cream, 1 tbsp powdered sugar

1. Crush biscuits roughly with a rolling pin (belan) by placing them in a polythene. Transfer to a bowl. Add milk & melted butter. Press biscuits at the base of a loose bottom tin of 8" diameter or a glass serving dish. Place in the fridge to set.
2. Place hung curd, paneer, cheese spread and powdered sugar in a mixer and blend to a very smooth paste. Check with the fingers to see that it is no longer grainy. Remove curd-paneer to a big mixing bowl.
3. Boil puree of 2 kiwis, 1½ cups water & 4 tbsp sugar in a pan, stirring continuously on low heat. Simmer for 1-2 minutes. Remove from fire.
4. Take ½ cup water in a pan. Sprinkle gelatine on it. Stir on low heat for 2 minutes till gelatine dissolves. Remove from fire and add to kiwi mix.
5. Add the kiwi mixture to the curd-paneer paste. Mix well. Add some colour if required. Place in the freezer for 15 minutes or till slightly thick.
6. Remove cheese cake mix from the freezer and beat till smooth. If using eggs, fold in stiff egg whites gently with a spoon. Pour over the biscuit base. Keep in the fridge (not freezer) for 3-4 hours to set.
7. For topping, soak gelatine in ½ cup water. Heat on low flame, stirring continuously till gelatine dissolves. Add kiwi puree & sugar. Cook for 1 min on low heat. Remove from fire. Add enough colour & bring down to room temperature.
8. Spoon glaze over the set cheese cake. Keep it in the fridge to set.
9. Pipe stars with whipped cream. Take 75 gm of cream in a cold pan, 1 tbsp powdered sugar & ½ tsp lime juice. Beat on ice till thick & can stand in firm peaks. Put in icing bag & pipe stars on cheese cake. Serve cold, cut into wedges.

Hyderabadi Dum Biryani: Recipe on page 110, Vegetable Seekh: Recipe on page 15 ➤

BEST SELLER BY *Nita Mehta* (Non-Vegetarian)

TANDOORI
COOKING in the OVEN

The Best of
NON-VEGETARIAN

The Best of
CHICKEN & PANEER

Simply Delicious
CURRIES

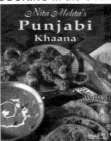

PUNJABI Khaana

MUGHLAI Khaana

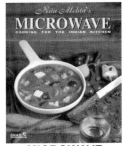

MICROWAVE
COOKING FOR THE INDIAN KITCHEN

BAKES & CAKES
Baking with Confidence!

CHINESE
cooking for the Indian kitchen

CONTINENTAL
cooking for the Indian kitchen

ITALIAN
cooking for the Indian kitchen

Tempting SNACKS

Favourite
NON VEGETARIAN Dishes

CONTINENTAL
Non-Vegetarian

MUGHLAI
NonVeg Khaana

Flavours of INDIAN COOKING
(All Colour)

LOW CALORIE RECIPES

The Best of **CHICKEN**

THAI COOKERY

PUNJABI NonVeg

BREAKFAST NonVeg

ITALIAN NonVeg

Taste of KASHMIR

CHINESE COOKERY

OVEN Recipes NonVeg

SNACKS NonVeg

MICROWAVE Cookery

The Best of MUTTON

MORE CHICKEN

LOW CALORIE
cooking for the Indian kitchen

BEST SELLER BY *Nita Mehta* (Vegetarian)

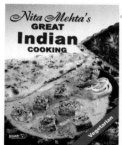
Great INDIAN Cooking

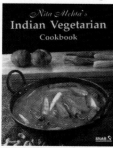
INDIAN Vegetarian Cookbook

Vegetarian SNACKS

QUICK Vegetarian Cooking

INTERNATIONAL
cooking for the Indian kitchen

Perfect Vegetarian Cookery

SUBZIYAAN
Tasty VEGETABLES for EVERYDAY Cooking

Vegetarian Wonders

Vegetarian CURRIES

ITALIAN
Vegetarian Cookery

Low Calorie Desserts

DESSERTS

TANDOORI
Cooking in the OVEN

FOOD FOR CHILDREN

Eggless OVEN Recipes

All Time Favourite
SNACKS

MORE SNACKS

CAKES &
CHOCOLATES

CONTINENTAL
Vegetarian Cookery

Soups Salads Starters

ZERO OIL

Low Calorie Recipes

LOW FAT Tasty Recipes

ICE-CREAMS

The Art of BAKING

Taste of RAJASTHAN

LOSE WEIGHT

PRESSURE COOKING

SANDWICHES

DINNER MENUS from
Around the World

Great Ideas-
COOKING TIPS

NITA MEHTA COOKERY CLASSES
Starts 15Th of Every Month (4 Day Course)
CALL TO REGISTER: 26214011, 26238727, 23250091, 23252948 (DELHI)

Map of Contemporary Ireland

NORTHERN IRELAND

DONEGAL

SLIGO

MAYO

LEITRIM

ROSCOMMON

CAVAN

MONAGHAN

LONGFORD

LOUTH

GALWAY

WESTMEATH

MEATH

DUBLIN

REPUBLIC

OF

IRELAND

OFFALY

KILDARE

CLARE

LAOIS

WICKLOW

CARLOW

LIMERICK

TIPPERARY

KILKENNY

WEXFORD

KERRY

WATERFORD

CORK

DISTRICTS OF NORTHERN IRELAND:

1	DERRY CITY	14	CARRICKFERGUS
2	LIMAVADY	15	FERMANAGH
3	COLERAINE	16	DUNGANNON
4	BALLYMONEY	17	CRAIGAVON
5	MOYLE	18	LISBURN
6	STRABANE	19	BELFAST CITY
7	MAGHERAFELT	20	CASTLEREAGH
8	BALLYMENA	21	ARDS
9	LARNE	22	ARMAGH
10	OMAGH	23	BANBRIDGE
11	COOKSTOWN	24	DOWN
12	ANTRIM	25	NEWRY AND MOURNE
13	NEWTOWNABBEY	26	NORTH DOWN

ANCIENT
IRELAND

ANCIENT IRELAND

Iain Zaczek

PHOTOGRAPHY BY
David Lyons

First published in Great Britain in 1998 by
Collins and Brown Limited
London House, Great Eastern Wharf
Parkgate Road, London SW11 4NQ

1 3 5 7 9 8 6 4 2

British Library Cataloguing-in-Publication Data:
A catalogue record for this title is
available from the British Library.

ISBN 1 85585 4945 (hardback edition)
ISBN 1 85585 6107 (paperback edition)

Conceived, edited and designed by
Collins & Brown Limited

Editorial Director Sarah Hoggett
Art Director Roger Bristow
Editor Lisa Balkwill
Designer Bill Mason
Map by Andrew Farmer

Printed and bound in Italy

JACKET ILLUSTRATIONS:

FRONT: Co. Antrim, Glenaan, Neolithic court
cairn of St Ossian's grave.
BACK: Co. Kerry, Dingle Peninsula, beehive hut.

HALF TITLE: Co. Wicklow, Glendalough, St Kevin's Church.

TITLE: Co. Clare, the cliffs of Moher.

ACKNOWLEDGMENTS

David Lyons – My thanks to:
The numerous people I have encountered over the years whilst
photographing in the temples, tomb sites and farm fields throughout
Ireland for their kindness, patience and conversation.

I am particularly indebted to Aida Monsell and Ronan Whelan at
the Department of Arts, Culture and the Gaeltacht, Dublin, for
helping to open some doors, and to Maria O'Connell for applying a
little Chicago-style efficiency to a stubborn photographer.

Thanks also to my family in Bushmills for putting up with me and
providing 'base camp' once again, and my gratitude to Duncan
Harrison of Positive Image, Leeds, who has processed my films for
many years with dependable care.

And to quote the blessing of the man on the banks of the
Shannon,
'*May they be in Heaven a week before the Devil knows
they're dead.*'

Contents

MAP OF ANCIENT IRELAND

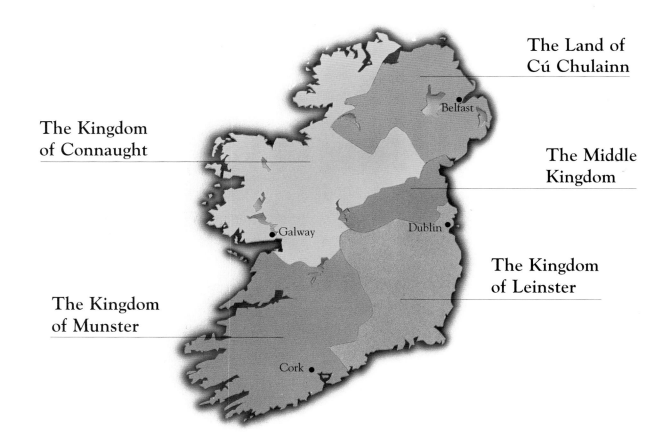

The Land of
Cú Chulainn

Belfast

The Kingdom
of Connaught

The Middle
Kingdom

Galway

Dublin

The Kingdom
of Leinster

The Kingdom
of Munster

Cork

INTRODUCTION

ANY TRAVELLER IN Ireland will swiftly come to appreciate the rich diversity of the landscape. Around the Leinster plains and the foothills of the Wicklow mountains, there are stretches of rolling pastureland, as green and fertile as any farmer could wish. Along the Antrim and Donegal coastline in the north, and the Dingle peninsula in Munster, there are fine views and rocky promontories, buffeted by squalling winds and choppy seas. Inland, around Lough Erne and the banks of the winding Shannon, there are mazy clusters of lakes and wetlands, dotted with tiny, grassy islands. In the central lowlands the scene is dominated by thick tracts of peat and bogland, abounding in native wildlife. Then again, in Co. Clare, there is the strange lunar landscape of the Burren, with its bleak limestone plateau.

Each of these features presented different challenges and opportunities for Ireland's early inhabitants, helping to shape the way that they left their mark upon the landscape. At the most basic level, they determined the types of dwellings and monuments that they could build, along with the kinds of skills they could develop. It was no accident, for example, that a prehistoric axe 'factory' developed in the Antrim area, since the best seams of porcellanite rock – the preferred material for axe-heads – were discovered on the slopes of Tievebulliagh mountain. Similarly, it is clear that beehive huts and stone cashels were much more common in the rocky districts of the south-west, than in the more fertile areas of the east and north.

The same practicalities apply to matters of defence. Because of the comparative flatness of its terrain, hillforts were less common in Ireland than in countries such as Britain. Instead, early inhabitants looked for other possibilities in the landscape. Promontory forts were popular, as the rocky Irish coastline provided a natural defence against potential attackers. Inland, there was often a tendency to make use of waterlogged sites. In loughs and in marshy areas, chieftains would fortify tiny islands or construct their own artificial islands (crannógs), surrounding them with timber palisades. This practice continued long into the Middle Ages, when castles were often situated on islands.

More important still was the question of food. The people from Ireland's most ancient site, the Mesolithic settlement at Mount Sandel, Co. Kerry (c. 7000 BC) were hunter-gatherers, surviving on a diet of salmon, eels, duck and nuts. They may have been largely nomadic, but their successors created more permanent homes. They were farmers who also raised livestock and practised the skills of pottery and weaving. Naturally, they

sought out the best land for their crops – usually opting for soil with good drainage and avoiding peaty and low-lying areas. Very little remains of their dwellings, which were made of perishable materials, although the Neolithic huts at Lough Gur (*c.* 2750 BC, p. 120–121) provide a rare exception.

These farmers also erected Ireland's great megalithic monuments, and their disposition gives the best clue to the settlements of the Neolithic population. The stone monuments date from the 4th millennium BC, with certain parts of Carrowmore (*c.* 3290 BC) and Newgrange (*c.* 3200 BC) being among the oldest. Most were communal burial places, although a few had more elaborate ritual and astronomical functions.

In essence, there were four main types of monument: court cairns, portal tombs or dolmens, passage-graves and wedge tombs. Court cairns, chamber tombs with semi-circular forecourts, were probably the earliest (see Ossian's grave, p. 53). They are restricted almost exclusively to northern areas. Portal tombs, which grace the landscape with their spectacular balancing acts, are believed to have evolved out of these. They are mainly found in the north, although there are a few examples in southern Leinster. The decorated passage-graves, the finest of all the Irish monuments, are thought to have been erected by people who came from Brittany and who landed in the river Boyne region before heading west.

By the start of the Bronze Age (*c.* 2000 BC) the emphasis seems to have shifted to simple wedge-tombs. The climate also became warmer during this period, leading to the spread of peat and bog over large areas of cultivated land, ruining the agricultural experiments at places like the Céide Fields (p. 24).

The Iron Age saw the arrival of the Celts in Ireland. They originated as a group of loosely-connected tribes in central Europe in around 600 BC. During the course of the La Tène period (*c.* 450 BC–*c.* 50 BC), they pushed westwards, partly through pressure from the expanding Roman empire. Their presence in Ireland may date from the 3rd century BC.

The Celts themselves viewed their early history as a series of invasions by five different races who migrated to Ireland during its historic period. These were the Partholónians, the Nemedians, the Fir Bolg, the Tuatha Dé Danaan and the Milesians. The first two groups are unidentifiable, but the Fir Bolg have been linked with the Belgae, a continental tribe of mixed Germanic and Celtic stock. They began migrating to Britain in the 1st century BC, and could have reached Ireland a century or so later. A longstanding tradition links them with the construction of some promontory forts such as Dun Aenghus (see p. 27). The Tuatha Dé Danaan were the Irish gods, led by the Dagda. According to ancient belief, it was this divine race of beings who constructed the great prehistoric mounds, to serve as palaces after they were swept from power by the Milesians. The latter have a much firmer grounding in reality and are thought to represent the ancestors of the Gaels.

LEFT: LOWERLOUGH ERNE, CO. FERMANAGH

The lake's tiny, wooded islands were a favourite haunt of hermits and holy men, such as St Molaise. His name is also linked with retreats at Inishmurray, Co.Sligo, and on the Scottish island of Arran.

Further hints about Ireland's past can be gleaned from its two ancient series of tales, the Ulster cycle and the Fionn, or Fenian, cycle. The first of these was set in the 1st century BC and its background details offer revealing insights into Iron Age society. At its heart was the rivalry between Ulster and Connaught, at a time when Tara and the Middle Kingdom had not yet risen to prominence. Instead the focus was on the northern centres of royal power, Emain Macha (now Navan Fort, p. 52) and Cruachan (now Rathcroghan). The complex remains at Navan Fort, where a series of elaborate structures were ritually destroyed by fire, suggest that 'royal' sites were more akin to shrines than strongholds.

The same cannot be said of the sites associated with the warrior heroes. The home of Cú Chulainn, the hero of the Ulster cycle, was specified as Dun Dealgan (now Dundalk). The 'dun' in this instance simply means fort, as in Dun Aenghus or Dunbeg. Surviving examples do not appear to be any more imposing than other types of fort, such as cashels or raths, but the name is used more sparingly, implying that it was reserved for places of some prestige.

The Fionn cycle of stories describes the adventures of Finn Mac Cool and his valiant knights, the Fianna. They are set in a later age, the 3rd century AD, and the social background is often blurred by subsequent Christian additions to the text. Even so, it is noticeable that Finn, very much a hero of Leinster, regards the high king at Tara as the supreme authority.

During this time Ireland's people were grouped together in *tuatha* (tribes or clans) which were ruled over by a king (*rí*).

Some kings were little more than petty chieftains, while others controlled several *tuatha*. At the top of the hierarchy, there was a high king (*ard rí*). These units were strengthened by ties of kinship which were complicated by widespread polygamy and an elaborate system of fosterage. These various measures helped to compensate for the lack of a strong, central organization, although they also gave rise to a host of inter-tribal squabbles. Worse still, they left the Irish ill-equipped to act in unison, when they were faced with their Viking and Norman foes.

Few details are known of the tribes that existed before the 5th century AD. The oldest names generally relate to animals – among them the Osraige (deer-people) and the Sordraige (boar-people) – and probably refer to their tribal gods. By the start of the early historic period, however, specific dynasties were beginning to emerge, each stemming from a powerful ancestor figure. In the pre-Viking period, the most influential of these were the Eoghanacht, the Connachta and the Uí Néill. The latter were usually dominant enough to hold the high kingship of Tara, even though this rarely brought them anything more than nominal overlordship of their rivals.

Most tribes dwelt in scattered farms and homesteads. The chief and his wealthier subjects might have lived in a crannóg (fortified lake-dwelling) or in one of the larger cashels. The remainder would have occupied the smaller ringforts or timber huts which have long since disappeared. In the rocky areas of the south-west, clocháns (beehive huts) were another option. Most of these dwellings are notoriously difficult to date. Some archaeologists assign them to the Iron Age, while others argue that they are early medieval. The styles, it seems, changed remarkably little over the centuries and there is a surprising dearth of documentary evidence.

The most unusual feature of the Irish social system was the absence of towns and villages. This had a telling effect on the way that Christianity was introduced into the country. The organization of the Roman Church, which was structured around the bishop and his diocese, proved unsuitable for such a diffuse community. Monasteries, on the other hand, fared much better. They became the spiritual equivalent of the *tuath*, rapidly acquiring a semi-independent character. Their buildings did not, as yet, follow the well-ordered continental model. Rather, they resembled a haphazard settlement, as the remains at Glendalough (p. 156) confirm. Even so, religious houses were carefully sited. Abbots ensured that communications were good and that the land was suitable for livestock or crops. In addition, monasteries were invariably close to the stronghold of a powerful secular lord, whether for reasons of patronage or protection. Accordingly, most of the major foundations were located in central or eastern Ireland.

In contrast, early Christian hermits chose to live in remote, isolated spots. They did so in a spirit of self-sacrifice, for this was a period when any man who left his tribe was deprived of both his legal and social identity. Some idea of this spartan existence can be gained from the remains at Skellig Michael and the Gallarus oratory (p. 129), although many of the sites were later turned into churches, as at Dysert O'Dea. Others were looted and abandoned after the Norsemen began to arrive.

The monasteries, meanwhile, became important artistic centres. Magnificent illuminated manuscripts were produced in the monastic workshops, while the altars gleamed with displays of ornate liturgical vessels and reliquaries. Sadly for the monks, these riches attracted the attention of Viking marauders and many of them ended up as booty, carried back to the longships. Only the heavy stone crosses, which adorned the monastery precincts, were spared this indignity.

The first Viking raid on Irish soil took place in 795. At first, these attacks were small-scale affairs carried out by minor warlords. Then, as the lack of serious resistance became evident, the violence escalated. By the 830s, the Norsemen were despatching huge floating fortresses which they moored in rivers like the Boyne and Liffey and then used as departure points for inland raids. Armagh, Kildare and Glendalough were all pillaged, before the Norsemen turned their attention to the creation of permanent settlements. Many of Ireland's major cities – Dublin, Cork, and Limerick among them – were founded in this way. The Irish response to the invasion was muted. Inter-tribal warfare continued unabated and, after a time, the Viking settlements became participants in these struggles. This state of affairs continued until the end of the 10th century when Brian Boru finally managed to mount a serious challenge to the invaders. His victory at Clontarf (1014) is usually cited as the closing episode in Ireland's Viking saga.

More than any of his predecessors, Brian managed to inject a real sense of power and authority into the role of high king. Much of this work was soon undone, as the provincial rulers returned to their old animosities. This reached a dangerous pitch in the 12th century, when the Connaught-born high king, Turlough O'Connor, tried to bolster his position by dividing up Meath and Munster. His son, Rory O'Connor, continued in the same vein by attacking King Dermot of Leinster and expelling him from his castle. Dermot swiftly fled to Henry II of England, appealing to him for help. Henry, who had already secured papal backing for an invasion, helped Dermot to return to

BELOW: MUIREDACH'S CROSS, MONASTERBOICE, CO. LOUTH

The carvings on some Celtic crosses mirror the grotesque decoration found in Irish manuscripts. Here, two cats devour a bird and frog.

Ireland with a force of men, led by Strongbow, the Earl of Pembroke. Victory followed immediately and, throughout the 1170s, waves of Norman adventurers sailed across to Ireland, eager to make their fortunes. Alarmed at their success, Henry reserved a strip of land on the eastern seabord – soon to become known as the English Pale – while allowing his barons to take what they could of the remainder. This they did with brutal efficiency. In 1183, Rory O'Connor gave up the struggle and retired to the Abbey of Cong. He was the last to hold the post of high king and, with his passing, Ireland's most important link with the past was broken.

In ancient times, Ireland had stood at the very edge of the known world. The people who journeyed there were pioneers, whether they were warriors seeking out new lands or hermits looking for a peaceful haven. The signs of their endeavours can still be found, half-hidden in the tucks and folds of the landscape. From the majestic remains of prehistoric tombs and ringforts to the modest shells of beehive huts and farmsteads, the memories of a distant past live on, conjured up by the beautiful photographs on these pages.

The five chapters in this book reflect the *cóiceda* or 'fifths', the independent provinces recognized by the ancient Celts. These were Connaught, Ulster (the land of Cú Chulainn), the Middle Kingdom of Meath, Munster and Leinster.

RIGHT: NORTH CROSS, AHENNY, CO. TIPPERARY

The design of this cross was probably inspired by Celtic metalwork of the period. The five studs may be the equivalents of the original rivets.

THE KINGDOM OF
CONNAUGHT

CONNAUGHT IS named after Conn Cétchathach (Conn of the Hundred Battles), one of the ancient high kings. He is supposed to have lived during the 2nd century AD and was the founder of a dynasty; his descendants became known as the Connachta. In 137 he participated in the battle of Magh Léana, a conflict that pitted him against Eoghan of Munster and is said to have led to the division of Ireland into two kingdoms, the north and the south.

The original province of Connaught played a major part in the legends of the Ulster cycle, the ancient tales from Ireland's heroic age. These stories are thought to be set in the 1st century BC, but they were transmitted orally for many hundreds of years and became modified in the process.

LEFT: DERRYCLARE LOUGH, CONNEMARA, CO. GALWAY

Connemara is sometimes thought to take its name from Conmac, the son of Maeve and Fergus. Maeve was the queen of Connaught and Fergus was an exiled Ulster warrior.

ABOVE: CARROWMORE, CO. SLIGO

Grave 7 is one of the best preserved graves at the megalithic cemetary of Carrowmore. Dating back to c. 3290 BC, it stands at the centre of a circle of 31 stones and contains the remains of four cremation burials between its uprights.

The chief story in the Ulster cycle was the epic *Táin Bó Cuailnge* (*Cattle Raid of Cooley*). This described a bitter war that was waged between Ulster and Connaught over the possession of an enchanted bull. During this campaign Connaught's forces were led by Medb and her consort King Ailill against the Ulster warrior Cú Chulainn (see p. 47). Medb was frequently anglicized as Maeve and in this form she has been linked with a

number of prehistoric monuments, most notably the burial mound near Carrowmore (see left and pp. 22–23).

Maeve was originally a goddess of war and sovereignty, and in this latter guise was involved in ritual matings with kings at the sacred sites of Tara and Cruachan, Connaught's ancient capital now identified as Rathcroghan (Rath of Cruachan) in County Roscommon. Along with Newgrange and Tailte, Cruachan was famed as one of the three sacred cemeteries of prehistoric times; it was also thought to possess a hidden gateway to the Otherworld.

The fact that Maeve was linked with both Tara and Cruachan tallies well with early historic developments. It is widely believed that the Connachta were the ancestors of Niall Noígiallach (Niall of the Nine Hostages), one of the first kings of Tara, and his descendants the Uí Néill, the dynasty which came to dominate most of northern Ireland. It seems that they rose to prominence in the 5th century, sweeping aside the power of the Ulster people and seizing Tara from the tribes of Leinster. This appears to have coincided with a time when the Connachta were pushing eastwards, out of their traditional homeland. The legend that Niall was the youngest son of a Connaught king and a British slave-girl tends to support this theory, for his status would have forced him to carve out new territories for himself.

As time passed, the Connachta divided into three main branches. These were the Uí Maine, who controlled the area to the south of Lough Corrib; the Uí Briúin, who settled in the neighbouring land; and the Uí Fiachrach, who were based in northern Mayo. The kingship tended to rotate between these last two groups, with neither dynasty managing to hold onto power for very long.

Notable leaders of the Uí Briúin included Aed (d. 577), who fought at the battle of Cúil Dreimne, and Rogallach (d. 649), who seized the kingship after the battle of Canbo (622). Among the Uí Fiachrach, meanwhile, the most powerful ruler appears to have been Guaire (d. 663), who managed to beat off challenges to his throne in 653 and 654.

During the Christian period, the key figure in Connaught was St Enda (d. c. 530) who trained at St Ninian's monastery at Whithorn, Galloway. His chief foundation was at Inishmore on the Aran Islands, where the monastic school produced distinguished pupils such as St Ciaran, the founder of the monastery of Clonmacnois.

In the secular sphere, the Connachta were eventually superseded by the O'Connors. Their leading figure was Turlough O'Connor, who became king of the province in 1106 and high king in 1119. He embarked upon a non-stop series of campaigns, resulting in Munster's division into Thomond and Desmond, with one section going to the O'Briens and the other to the Mac

Carthys. In Meath he pursued a similar policy, dividing the kingdom into three parts and stoking up the traditional rivalry between it and Leinster. O'Connor was scarcely less active in matters of religion. He made generous donations to Cong, Co. Mayo, commissioning its famous cross, and raised the profile of the church at Tuam in Co. Galway, to such an extent that it was made an archbishopric at the Synod of Kells (1152).

Unfortunately for the province, Turlough O'Connor's successor did not inherit his abilities and the divisions which had been created offered a tempting opportunity for the Normans. Rory O'Connor proved to be the country's last high king, eventually retiring to Cong in 1183. By this time the Anglo-Norman invasion was in full flow, as waves of adventurers crossed the Irish Sea to make their fortunes. Connaught, however, did not feel the brunt of this until after the 1230s, when the de Burgos became the dominant lords in the area.

LEFT: GREENCASTLE, CO. DONEGAL

Also known as Northburgh or Newcastle, Greencastle was built by Richard de Burgo, the 'Red' Earl of Ulster, in 1305. It fell to Edward Bruce in 1316, but was recaptured by de Burgo two years later.

CARVED FACE, CARNDONAGH, CO. DONEGAL

Left: EARLY MISSIONARIES used to Christianize the prehistoric stones they found by carving a simple cross on them. Gradually they became more ambitious, hiring artists to sculpt complex Biblical scenes on their Celtic crosses. The carvings at Carndonagh mark a very early stage in this process, as they were among the first to feature human figures.

CARVED 'STATION' PILLAR, GLENCOLUMBKILLE, CO. DONEGAL

Right: THE VALLEY of Glencolumbkille takes its name from St Columba, who is said to have confronted a demon here. In commemoration of this, a special *turas*, 'pilgrimage', is held on the saint's feast day. This entails sending worshippers on a 4.8-kilometre (3-mile) trek to visit 15 different 'stations', similar to the Christian Stations of the Cross. Most of these are either prehistoric sites or rock formations, such as Columcille's Chair. The route to the different stations is marked by a series of early cross-slabs or pillars.

KILCLOONEY PORTAL DOLMENS, CO. DONEGAL

NOT FAR FROM ARDARA, stands a pair of portal dolmens,
popularly known as the beds of Diarmaid and Gráinne.
They were the subject of one of the most famous stories in Irish
mythology. Gráinne was due to marry Finn Mac Cool, the
warrior hero of Irish legend, but shortly after the betrothal feast
she eloped with Diarmaid, a leading warrior under Finn's
command. For 16 years, Finn pursued the couple relentlessly,
forcing them to take shelter in a series of forests, caves and
remote hiding-places before they were finally rescued by
Oenghus, the god of love.

Carrowmore, Co. Sligo

Right: THE MEGALITHIC CEMETERY at Carrowmore may once have been the largest in Europe. A century ago, more than a hundred graves were still in existence here, but this number has now dwindled alarmingly. One of the best-preserved examples is grave 7, in the foreground, parts of which date back to *c.* 3290 BC. Consisting of a polygonal chamber, it is surrounded by a ring of boulders. In the background is a huge cairn, traditionally known as Maeve's Lump. This commemorates the supernatural queen of Connaught, who waged war against Cú Chulainn in the *Cattle Raid of Cooley.*

CÉIDE FIELDS, CO. MAYO

Above: HIDDEN UNDER A bleak stretch of moorland, close to the
north Mayo coastline, are the remains of Europe's largest-known prehistoric
farming settlement. Apparently planned as a single enterprise and run on a
communal basis, it is criss-crossed by a huge network of stone-walled
enclosures. The settlement survived until a gradual change in climate
buried the fields beneath a layer of bogland.

RATHFRAN WEDGE-TOMB, CO. MAYO

Above: WEDGE-SHAPED GALLERY GRAVES are the most common
form of megalithic monument in Ireland. Almost 400 examples are
known, most of them concentrated in the west of the country.
They consist of long, rectangular chambers, which are wider and
higher at the front. Usually these chambers are covered with
capstones, although these are missing at Rathfran.

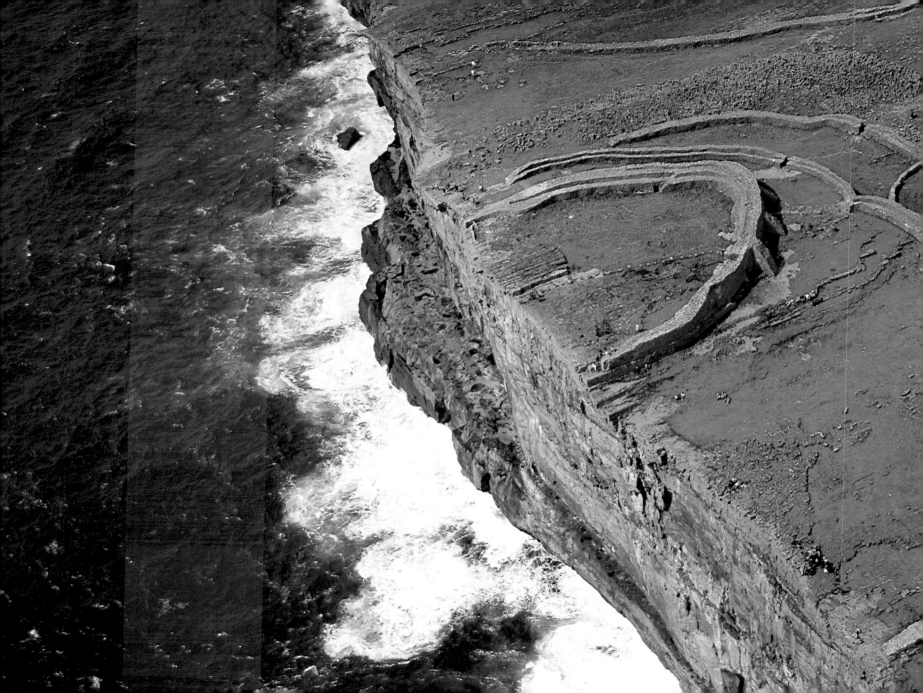

DUN AENGHUS, ARAN ISLANDS, CO. GALWAY

Left: WITH ITS SPECTACULAR position, crowning the
summit of a vertical cliff-face, Dun Aenghus is the finest
of the Irish promontory forts. Its walls are 4 metres
(12 feet) thick in places, and access to the inner
enclosure could only be gained through three narrow
gaps. The most formidable aspect of its defence,
however, was the *chevaux-de-frise,* 'Friesian horses',
a ring of tightly packed stone spikes hugging the curves
of the second wall. Legend ascribes the building of Dun
Aenghus to the Firbolg, a mythical people sometimes
associated with the Belgae, distant ancestors of the
Belgians. Archaeological finds within the fort suggest
that it may date back to the Celtic Iron Age.

THE TUROE STONE, CO. GALWAY

Left: THIS DOMED GRANITE monolith, is covered in a series of flowing, tendril patterns, which link it with the art of the prehistoric La Tène period. Similar motifs can be found on the metalwork produced by the ancient Celts. The stone is situated near a ringfort and burial site, but its elaborate design and phallic shape suggest that it served a ritual purpose.

FINN MAC COOL'S FINGER STONE, EASKY, CO. SLIGO

Right: ALSO KNOWN SIMPLY as the Split Rock, this is one of a number of monuments named after the legendary hero, Finn Mac Cool. He was the Irish equivalent of King Arthur, the leader of a band of valiant knights called the Fianna. According to legend, Finn could foresee the future when he sucked his thumb, a power which he gained after burning it on the magical Salmon of Knowledge.

Inishowen Peninsula, Co. Donegal

Left: THE WAVES ROLL IN near Malin Head, the most northerly point of Ireland on the Inishowen Peninsula. This stretch of coastline boasts several ancient monuments, most notably the chamber tombs at Malin and Carrowmore, and the promontory forts of Dunargus and Dungolgan. The chief attraction on the peninsula, however, is the ivy-clad ruin of Greencastle (see p. 17). This was erected in 1305 by Richard de Burgo, the 'Red' Earl of Ulster, in the hope that it would cement Norman power in the region. These ambitions were short-lived, as the castle was seized by Edward Bruce, the brother of Robert Bruce, just a decade later.

CHRISTIAN PILLAR-STONES, CARNDONAGH, CO. DONEGAL

BEFORE THE TRADITIONAL design of the Celtic cross evolved,
Irish artists used to carve religious scenes onto shaped stone
slabs. The examples at Carndonagh are among the earliest,
perhaps dating back as far as the 7th century. One figure
(detail, right), possibly a pilgrim, carries a bell, book and staff.
Another (left) holds a harp and has been tentatively identified
as King David, the author of the Psalms. The large 'marigold'
cross (far left) is thought to be a stylized version of a
flabellum, a liturgical fan.

INISHMORE, ARAN ISLANDS, CO. GALWAY

Right: MANY IRISH MONKS desired nothing more than to seek out some remote and inaccessible spot, where they could devote themselves to a life of manual labour and prayer. The Aran Islands were a favourite choice and Inishmore – the largest of the islands – is covered in early Christian sites. The holiest of these was Tighlagheany, 'Enda's Household', dedicated to the 5th–6th century saint, who was granted the archipelago by King Aenghus of Munster. Enda's churchyard is said to contain the graves of 120 saints, including his own, along with the remains of a decorated cross-shaft (left). In the north of the island, the mis-named 'Seven Churches' are dedicated to St Brecan, although it is likely they include a number of domestic buildings.

Sligo Bay, Co. Sligo

Right: THIS IS MAEVE'S REALM by the sea, pictured
from the legendary site of her grave at Knocknarea. In
early legend, she was the cruel queen of Connaught who
sent her armies to war for the sake of a magic bull. At
other times, she was portrayed as a goddess of war and
sovereignty. She had the ability to change her shape at
will, to run with the speed of a horse, and to sap her
enemies of their strength. Her power even extended to
Tara, where the high kings were obliged to mate with
her before they were allowed to rule.

CONG ABBEY, CO. MAYO

Above: CONG ABBEY STANDS on the site of an ancient monastery, founded in the 7th century by St Fechin. This was taken over by the Augustinians in the early 12th century, a generous endowment by King Turlough O'Connor. Its profile was raised even further at the end of the century when it became the refuge of Rory O'Connor, the last high king.

Cong is most famous for its Celtic processional cross, which is now displayed in Dublin's National Museum. Perhaps the most interesting of the surviving buildings is the charming riverside fishing-house (right). The monks rigged up an ingenious system here, so that a bell rang in the kitchen whenever a fish was caught.

SLIEVE LEAGUE, CO. DONEGAL

Right: STORMY WATERS CHURN around at the foot of
Europe's tallest sea-cliffs. These rise to a majestic 601
metres (1,972 feet) above the Atlantic. Not surprisingly,
the sheer inaccessibility of the place attracted a number
of hermits. Chief among these were St Assicus and
St Aodh Mac Bric, whose dwelling-place is now marked
by a ruined oratory and a holy well. St Assicus was
known by the nickname of 'St Patrick's goldsmith', while
St Aodh was both a physician and a former prince of the
Uí Néill, the main Ulster dynasty of rulers. His name
was invoked by those suffering from headaches.

DOORWAY DETAIL, CLONFERT CATHEDRAL, CO. GALWAY

Right: In 558, a monastery was founded here by St Brendan, on a site called Cluain Fhearta, 'the Field of the Grave'. By the standards of his time, Brendan travelled widely – he visited St Columba in Iona and St Malo in Brittany – and this inspired a 10th-century monk to attribute a series of imaginary voyages to him. The book became a medieval bestseller, attracting many pilgrims to the original location of the saint's shrine. This may explain why the authorities commissioned such an elaborately carved entrance for the church.

MERMAID, CLONFERT CATHEDRAL, CO. GALWAY

Left: CARVINGS OF MERMAIDS were commonplace in medieval churches, where they represented the sins of lust and debauchery. This image was particularly powerful in Ireland, because of the ancient legend that St Patrick had turned pagan women into mermaids before banishing them. In addition, Clonfert's close association with Brendan the Navigator made the marine theme even more appropriate.

LOUGH CORRIB, CO. GALWAY

Right: DRYSTONE WALLS, shown here winding their way down a grassy hillside towards the shores of Lough Corrib, have been popular for centuries, especially in areas with little tree shelter. Lough Corrib itself is studded with tiny islets, most of which are deserted, although a few bear reminders of Ireland's warring past. The finest of these island strongholds is Hen's Castle, so-called because of a legend that the owners kept a magic hen, which laid enough eggs to feed the entire garrison during one particular siege. The castle once belonged to the feuding O'Flaherty chieftains, whose name can be linked to several other forts in the area. Among these is Aughnanure Castle, which was originally built in 1256.

THE LAND OF
CÚ
CHULAINN

THE ANCIENT NAME of the northern *cóiced*,
or 'fifth', was Ulaid, which subsequently
developed into Ulster during the Viking age.
The ultimate source of this word is uncertain,
although there is a theory that it derived from
Ollamh (or Ollave) Fódhla, a legendary high king of
Ireland in the 8th century BC and the supposed
founder of the triennal festival at Tara (see p. 85).
Either way, the early history of the region was
undeniably complex, as its territorial boundaries and
the fortunes of its peoples shifted dramatically.

The high point of its influence occurred during
the heroic age. Although undoubtedly written from

LEFT: LOWER LOUGH ERNE, CO. FERMANAGH

*A westerly view of Lower Lough Erne, looking towards Donegal
Bay. The site of Devenish monastery is nearby.*

an Ulster perspective, the ancient tales about the exploits of the hero-warrior Cú Chulainn and his companions portrayed Ulaid as a large and powerful province. The Middle Kingdom had not yet been formed and most of its territories were under Ulster's control. Indeed, Cú Chulainn's home and the Cooley peninsula, where the main action of the Ulster cycle was set, are actually located in present-day Louth, and in the west Ulaid's influence appears to have extended as far south as Sligo Bay. At the heart of this mighty kingdom was the capital, Emain Macha, which archaeologists have linked with the important prehistoric site at Navan Fort (see p. 52). Its substantial remains emphasize that Emain Macha was once a place of both royal and sacred significance.

In the *Táin Bó Cuailnge* (*Cattle Raid of Cooley*), Cú Chulainn managed to protect Ulster from the armies of Connaught. In reality however the province was soon to be overrun and partitioned by its enemies. Traditionally, the first invasion was said to be the work of Cormac Mac Art, a high king who ruled in the 3rd century AD, but historical evidence suggests that it coincided with the emergence of the powerful Uí Néill dynasty two centuries later.

During the initial stages of Ulaid's decline, the central part of the province was occupied by a tribe known as the Airgialla

(subject peoples) and Emain Macha was destroyed, never to be rebuilt. Very little is known about this mysterious race of invaders. Some legends suggest that their attack was spearheaded by three brothers, the Collas, while others implicate three sons of Niall Noígiallach, one of sacred Tara's early kings. Either way, the Airgialla soon came to accept the overlordship of the Uí Néill and, shortly afterwards (*c.* 428), it was Donegal's turn to be conquered as Eoghan and Conall, two more of Niall's offspring, transformed it into the new kingdom of Ailech.

With this development, most of northern Ireland lay in the hands of the two main branches of the Uí Néill dynasty, ruling from their twin capitals at Ailech and Tara. The remaining Ulaid people were compressed into the north-eastern sectors of their original territory, where they held sway over a number of minor tribes. One of these, the Dál Riata, had the distinction of owning land in both Scotland and Ireland. The dynasty was descended from Fergus Mór, son of Erc, who prompted some of his followers to migrate to Scotland, where

LEFT: DEVENISH ISLAND, CO. FERMANAGH

The monastery on Devenish (Ox Island) was founded in the 6th century by St Molaise. The 25-metre (81-foot) round tower features a sculptured cornice.

they established a settlement between the kingdom of Strathclyde and Pictland. This move appears to have taken place in the first half of the 7th century, just as the Irish Dál Riata were coming under threat from the Uí Néill of Ailech.

It was against this volatile political background that St Patrick's mission to Ireland took place. It is not always easy to separate fact from fiction in the saint's life but even so, it does appear that many of the key events in Ireland's conversion took place on Ulster soil. During his youth, after he had been carried off to Ireland as a slave, Patrick received God's call at Mount Slemish, Co. Antrim, where he was tending flocks of sheep. Later, when he returned as a missionary, he landed at Strangford Lough, by the mouth of the Slaney river. Then, at Saul (see p. 67), he gained both his first church and his first convert, after winning over a pagan lord named Dichu with his preaching. Finally, and most important of all, it was at Armagh that he decided to establish his ecclesiastical capital.

Patrick built his new church just two miles away from Emain Macha. Its name derives from Ard Macha (Macha's Height), confirming its link with the ancient stronghold. Usually such a move would imply that the founder was seeking secular protection for his church. In this instance, Emain Macha was already in ruins, so it is more likely that Patrick wished to emphasize the contrast between the glory of the Christian Church and a symbol of defeated paganism.

In time, Armagh's links with the cult of St Patrick made it the most influential city in Ulster. This did not shield it from all its enemies, for the church was desecrated by the Vikings and

ABOVE: GIANT'S CAUSEWAY, CO. ANTRIM

The strange rock formations on the Giant's Causeway were created by a series of volcanic eruptions 60 million years ago. The lava cooled rapidly and as it did so, it shrank and cracked, leaving behind a honeycomb of hexagonal rocks.

looted three times by the Anglo-Normans. Even so, its prestige was raised in 1004 when Brian Boru, then king of all Ireland, acknowledged its primacy over the Irish Church, and again in 1152, when this was confirmed at the Synod of Kells.

Ulster also contained a number of Culdee churches, such as the Teampall Mór at Devenish. Culdee comes from the Irish *Céli dé* (servants of God) and refers to an austere group of settlements which flourished during the 8th and 9th centuries.

Giant's Causeway, Co. Antrim

Right: MANY LEGENDS HAVE attached themselves to this geological miracle. Most of them relate to the mythical hero, Finn Mac Cool. One story relates how a giant Finn built a bridge from Ireland to Staffa, in order to visit his beloved. The other end of this causeway was Fingal's Cave – Fingal being the Scottish version of his name. This ties in neatly with the facts, for the Giant's Causeway was created by a series of volcanic eruptions, which followed a vent stretching from Antrim to the island of Skye.

NAVAN FORT, CO. ARMAGH

Above: MOST AUTHORITIES equate this site with Emain Macha, the ancient seat of the kings of Ulster. According to legend, this gained its name when Macha, a horse-goddess, gave birth to twins, *'emhain'*, after racing the royal steeds. Here, too, King Conchobar held court at the time of Cú Chulainn's exploits against the Connaught army.

The historical Navan Fort was scarcely less distinguished. Excavations have revealed that a series of huge, wooden structures was erected here between *c.* 700–100 BC, protected by a circular stockade. Other finds include the skull of a Barbary ape, perhaps an exotic gift to the chieftain who presided here.

OSSIAN'S GRAVE, GLENAAN, CO. ANTRIM

Above: LOCAL LEGEND links this place with Ossian, a warrior hero whose adventures are related in the Fionn cycle of stories. He outlived his companions by travelling to Tir na Nog, the land of eternal youth, where he stayed for 300 years. Old age caught up with him however, when he set foot on Irish soil once more. In less fanciful terms, the stones form part of a Neolithic court cairn, a type of monument that is sometimes known as a 'lobster's claw', because its semi-circular row of stones is reminiscent of a pincer.

WHITE PARK BAY, CO. ANTRIM

Left: DURING THE NEOLITHIC AGE, when farmers
attempted to clear large tracts of wildwood, the axe was
a vital tool. The important axe 'factory' at Tievebulliagh,
a few miles south of White Park Bay, was the site of
many rich deposits of porcellanite rock. Northern
Antrim was a major source of production in this field,
and the axe-heads were brought here for polishing on
the basalt sand. There was a flourishing trade in
Tievebulliagh axes, and examples have been found as
far away as the Thames Valley, England. Using such a
tool, it has been shown that a man could fell a tree in
seven minutes and level 0.2 hectares (half an acre)
of scrubland within a week.

LEGANANNY DOLMEN, CO. DOWN

Left: SITUATED AT THE EDGE of the Mountains of Mourne region, this is one of the simplest portal dolmens, consisting of nothing more than three upright stones and a capstone. Its resemblance to an outsized table is apt, since the term 'dolmen' derives from two Breton words – *maen* and *taol*, which mean 'stone table'. This, in turn, may reflect old superstitions that dolmens were originally druid altars or giants' tables.

CRANNÓG, LOUGH NA CRANAGH, CO. ANTRIM

Right: CRANNÓGS ARE LAKE-DWELLINGS on artificial islands, mostly formed out of a mixture of brushwood and peat, ringed with a palisade of timber – hence the derivation of the term from *crann*, the Irish word for tree. This example is more elaborate, however, as the material is held in place by a stone wall. Most crannógs belonged to persons of high rank, as their construction required considerable manpower. They remained in common use for a remarkably long period of time, from the Neolithic era through to the late Middle Ages.

WHITE PARK BAY, CO. ANTRIM

Right: IT IS NOTORIOUSLY DIFFICULT to ascertain the lifestyle of prehistoric shore-dwellers because, ever since the 19th century, amateur collectors have disturbed sites and removed finds. Nevertheless, it is clear that White Park Bay was the focus of much activity. Some people lived in caves, while others built circular wooden huts, using stones at the base to wedge the logs into place. Smaller finds have consisted mainly of implements. The most commonplace are scrapers, curved pieces of flint used for smoothing wood or cleaning out animal hides. Hammers, awls and tranchets (sharpeners) have also come to light.

KILLADEAS, CO. FERMANAGH

Left: IN THE GRAVEYARD AT Killadeas there are three carved stones, dating back to the 8th or 9th century. The finest of them, known as the Bishop's Stone, portrays a stooping figure carrying a crozier and handbell. Both of these items were commonly associated with early Celtic saints and were frequently preserved as reliquaries.

LONGSHIP CARVING, DUNLUCE CASTLE, CO. ANTRIM

Right: THE GAUNT RUINS OF Dunluce Castle perch precariously upon a steep cliff-face. Its inhabitants were battered by the elements and once, many centuries ago, a violent storm sent the kitchen quarters crashing onto the rocks below. Bad weather was sometimes welcomed as it kept away the Viking longships – inspiring an unknown poet to pen the following lines:

Bitter is the wind tonight,
It tosses the ocean's white hair;
This night I do not fear the warriors of Norway
Coursing wildly on the Irish Sea.

SOUTERRAIN, DRUMENA CASHEL, CO. DOWN

FEMALE BATH-HOUSE, STRUELL WELLS, CO. DOWN

Left: IN COMMON WITH many other ringforts, the settlement at Drumena Cashel included a souterrain. This type of structure was a man-made underground gallery, lined with drystone slabs. Initially, a deep trench was dug, allowing the stone walls and lintels to be inserted. Then the passage was covered over, so that it was barely visible above ground. Souterrains were mainly used for storage purposes, although they could also act as refuges in times of danger. To this end, some souterrains contained hidden chambers.

Above: THIS BATH-HOUSE is one of four healing wells at Struell. The first provided drinking water, the second was for the eyes, and the remaining two were for bathing the limbs. By tradition, the waters owe their therapeutic powers to the fact that St Patrick himself used to bathe here. Accordingly, on Midsummer's Eve, ailing pilgrims would gather at St Patrick's Seat, a local rock formation, circle it seven times, and then immerse themselves in the healing waters.

BOA ISLAND, CO. FERMANAGH

Left: THE JANUS FIGURE, on Boa Island, was thought to serve a protective purpose, warding off evil from all sides. Boa Island took its name from Badb, the goddess of war and death, and the area remained an important druidic centre long after Christianity had taken root in other parts of Ireland. In the lakeside cemetery of Caldragh, remote and strange, two stone idols peer out from the undergrowth (right). The figures may date from the Christian era, but their inspiration is entirely pagan. The huge, pear-shaped faces – one of them a double-sided Janus head – carry echoes of the pillar-stones that were erected over some of the earliest Celtic grave-mounds.

WHITE ISLAND, CO. FERMANAGH

Above: THE MASK-LIKE faces and bulging eyes of these pillar carvings are characteristic of pagan Celtic sculpture, but these were probably designed for Christian churches.

SAUL, CO. DOWN

Left: THIS CHURCH was built to commemorate the site of 'Patrick's Barn', the first grant of land to be offered to the saint. Nothing remains of the original foundation, although there are two very ancient mortuary houses in the graveyard.

INCH ABBEY, CO. DOWN

Right: THE PICTURESQUE remains of Inch Abbey
are set on marshy land on the banks of the river Quoile.
Originally this was the site of a Celtic monastery, but
the place was sacked in 1002 by a band of Viking raiders.
Then, in 1180, the abbey was occupied by the Cistercian
monks of Carrick Abbey, whose home had been
destroyed. The land was bestowed by John de Courcy,
an Anglo-Norman freebooter who had effectively
established himself as an independent prince of Ulster.

BALLYNOE, CO. DOWN

Above: THE STONES AT BALLYNOE form an unusual burial site. Within the
outer ring is a low cairn, surrounded by a second row of boulders. Cist-graves
have been discovered at either end of the cairn, along with cremated remains
and some shards of Neolithic pottery. There is also a number of larger portal
stones, which are aligned towards the equinoctial sunset.

BONAMARGY FRIARY, BALLYCASTLE, CO. ANTRIM

Above: NEAR THE RESORT OF Ballycastle, the tranquil ruins of this old
Franciscan friary offer few hints of the district's troubled past. The MacDonnells
fought a pitched battle here with an English garrison, and many of the earls of
Antrim lie buried in the vault. In ancient legend too, the area was a place of ill
omen; the children of Lir were banished to this stretch of coastline for 300 years
after they were transformed into swans by their stepmother.

DRUMENA CASHEL, CO. DOWN

Left: IN ESSENCE, cashels are ringforts, which have walls made out of stone rather than earthworks. They are comparatively rare in Co. Down – only 57 have been detected – and their presence is largely confined to high, rocky areas, where deposits of stone were plentiful. The cashel at Drumena is one of the more straightforward examples. The outer wall is extremely thick, averaging around 3.4 metres (10½ feet), but there is no external ditch. It is composed of two layers of drystone, covering a core of rubble. Within the enclosure, excavations in the 1920s revealed a souterrain and traces of another drystone structure. The dating of cashels can only be very tentative, but this one is thought to have been built in the early Christian period.

GREY ABBEY, CO. DOWN

Right: GREY ABBEY IS one of the best-preserved Cistercian houses in the country. Its monks came from Holm Cultram in Cumbria and it was founded in 1193 by Affreca, the wife of John de Courcy (see pp. 68–69) and daughter of King Godred of Man. The Cistercians had a reputation for producing sober, restrained architecture, with a minimum of fussy decoration. Indeed their leader, St Bernard, made a point of denouncing the grotesque creatures found on so many romanesque churches. Instead, Grey Abbey is notable for its pioneering use of the gothic style, most evident in the elegant arch of the elaborate West door (left).

MONEA CASTLE, CO. FERMANAGH

Right: THE BRITISH CROWN attempted to establish a permanent presence in Ireland from the late 12th century, originally through a series of settlements known as 'plantations'. Early attempts to establish these in Munster and the Midlands were largely unsuccessful, but the policy fared better in Ulster. Monea Castle was built in 1618–19 by a planter, Malcolm Hamilton, the rector of Devenish. Memories of his original homeland appear to have been uppermost in his mind, for the striking barrel towers and crow-stepped gables lend a very Scottish air to the place.

DUNSEVERICK CASTLE, CO. ANTRIM

Left: DUNSEVERICK WAS built on the site of an ancient promontory fort, Dun Sobhairce, 'Sobhairce's fort'. Little is known of its early history, although it seems to have been important, as there was a road linking it directly to the holy site of Tara. The Vikings pillaged the place in 870 and 934, and the Irish, in turn, used it as a departure point for their raids on Scotland. St Patrick is said to have ordained St Olcán here, presenting him with the relics of the Apostles, Paul and Peter.

THE
MIDDLE
KINGDOM

THE MIDDLE KINGDOM was the most recently formed of the ancient divisions, the *cóiceda*, or 'fifths', and the only one that did not survive to become a modern province. It was centred around Mide (Meath) and was intended to act as a buffer-zone between the other warring lands. According to legend, it was founded in *c.* 130 AD by Tuathal Teachmhair, one of the early high kings. He chose the Hill of Ushnagh at Co. Westmeath (left), as the core of his new province, creating it from territories confiscated from the other districts.

For this reason the Hill of Ushnagh was often considered the mystical heart of Ireland. It was the

LEFT: THE HILL OF USHNAGH, CO. WESTMEATH

*The mystical centre of Ireland and once the site of a
pagan Beltane festival. Thirty-two counties are
said to be visible from its summit.*

setting for a major fire festival at Beltane, as well as the subject of a plethora of myths. The most exotic of these told how the wizard Merlin stole away with Ushnagh's impressive stone circle. Entering the place by moonlight, he uttered an incantation which caused the stones to uproot themselves and dance across the sea to England. There, they regrouped to form the circle of Stonehenge.

More than any other part of Ireland, the history of the Middle Kingdom was shaped by the splendour of its early monuments. In the sites of Newgrange and Tailte (now Teltown), it possessed two of the three great cemeteries of ancient times.

Tailte was named after the goddess Tailtu, the foster-mother of the sun god, Lugh. After her death he instituted the festival of Lughnasadh (a summer festival which falls on August 1st) and introduced a series of funeral games in her honour. These games, which were similar in concept to the Olympic Games, survived until the 12th century.

The grander monuments at Knowth (pp. 90–91) and Newgrange (pp. 86–89), persuaded locals that they were in the presence of gods, who resided in these stone temples. Newgrange, as the most impressive of the two monuments, was said to be the home of the Dagda, the father of the gods. In Irish myth, the gods were known as a race of ancient beings, known as the Tuatha Dé Danaan. They were thought to have ruled Ireland for many centuries until their defeat at the hands of a race called the Milesians. At this point, the Danaans retired to their *sidhe*, or fairy mounds, which were actually the burial mounds of prehistoric peoples. Although the *sidhe* appeared to be nothing more than simple, grassy mounds, legend has it that they concealed luxurious palaces where the gods devoted themselves to pleasure. A few ancient passage-graves featured carved decoration – such as the spiral motifs at Newgrange and the geometric patterns at Fourknocks (see p. 83) – indicating their significance as ritual sites. Other tombs, like the dolmen at Proleek (left), are more notable for their legendary associations.

LEFT: PROLEEK DOLMEN, CO. LOUTH

This dolmen is also known as the Giant's Load. Its name may refer to a nearby wedge-tomb, which belonged to a Scottish giant who crossed swords with Finn Mac Cool.

In historical terms the most influential prehistoric site in the Middle Kingdom was Tara (pp. 84–85). From a very early stage this was seen as the royal seat of the high kings, the most sacred place in pagan Ireland. Candidates were selected by the druids in a mystic ceremony known as the *tarbhfhess* (bull-sleep). After this, the prospective king had to participate in a ritual union with the earth-goddess. This *feis*, or ritual mating, was designed to ensure the prosperity of the land, since the fertility and wealth of the kingdom were thought to reflect the fortune and character of its ruler. This meant, among other things, that the king had to be free from any physical or moral blemish, and early storytellers related several tales about kings who were forced to abdicate after becoming scarred or disfigured in the course of a battle.

Tara was also the site of an important triennial festival which attracted chiefs, bards and historians from all parts of the land. At this assembly laws were passed, disputes were settled and clan genealogies were put on record. All enmities were laid aside during this period, and the event was celebrated with great feasting and music-making.

The historical realities of the high kingship of Tara are hard to assess. Ancient lists drawn up by the bards gave the names of 107 high kings before 1 AD, with a further 81 after that date, before the title disappeared in the 12th century. Most of these kings, however, were mythical; the first character of any real substance was Niall Noígiallach (Niall of the Nine Hostages), who appears to have lived during the early 5th century. Niall was the founder of the influential Uí Néill dynasty and gave his

ABOVE: FOURKNOCKS PASSAGE TOMB, CO. MEATH
Geometric design from the passage-grave at Fourknocks, which contained the remains of 65 people. Carvings of this kind are called scribings.

name to the Mound of the Hostages, one of the burial places at the seat of Tara.

Whether or not the high kingship entailed any real power is questionable, but it was certainly a source of prestige. Later rulers were eager to claim the title, although it only made them nominal overlords of other Irish chiefs.

The authority of Tara gradually declined under pressure from the Church, symbolized in the legendary battle between St Patrick and the high king. The Saint's triumph represented the victory of Christianity over the seat of pagan power.

THE ROYAL SEAT OF TARA, CO. MEATH

Left: TARA WAS THE HOLIEST SITE in ancient Ireland. It was the seat
of the high kings, where candidates were selected by the druids
in a mystical ceremony known as the *tarbhfhess* (bull-sleep).
These were confirmed at the Lia Fáil, the Stone of Destiny (right),
which was supposed to scream aloud when touched by the rightful
king. The importance of the site dates back to the Neolithic Age,
when the Mound of the Hostages – a monumental passage-grave –
was constructed. It was still revered centuries later, when the place
was seized by the Uí Néill dynasty, at the dawn of Irish history. Even
after this, Tara continued to exert its magic. In Christian lore, it was
said to be the site of a cursing contest between St Ruadhan and
Tara's pagan rulers, while medieval writers described a magnificent
Banqueting Hall, worthy of an Arthurian-style court. As recently as
1899, British Israelites explored the area, hoping to find traces
of the Ark of the Covenant.

PASSAGE TOMB, NEWGRANGE, CO. MEATH

Left: EARLY STORYTELLERS REGARDED Newgrange as a divine place, as it was the home of the Dagda, the father of the gods. It was stolen away from him by his son, Oenghus, who gave shelter to a runaway couple called Diarmaid and Gráinne (pp. 20–21) The heroine of this tale gave Newgrange (the Cave of Gráinne) its name. At dawn on the winter solstice, a thin shaft of sunlight enters through a specially constructed 'roof-box' and penetrates the entire length of the passage (right). Newgrange is also celebrated for its elaborate spiral designs (below), featured on the outer kerbstone and the inner walls of the tomb. In light of the monuments astronomical function, it is possible that they were meant to evoke the movement of the sun.

CORBELLED ROOF, NEWGRANGE, CO. MEATH

Right: IRELAND'S GREATEST prehistoric necropolis is the
Brug na Bóinne (Palace of the Boyne), a megalithic
complex situated a few miles west of Drogheda. At its
heart, there are three huge burial mounds – Newgrange,
Knowth and Dowth. Newgrange was occupied during
several different periods, although radiocarbon tests
suggest that the oldest parts may date back to around
3200 BC. The principal chamber rises to a height of
5.9 metres (19½ feet) and features a remarkable
funnel-shaped roof, created with early corbelling
techniques. This tomb was plundered in 862, when a
local princeling brought Norse raiders to the site.
Shortly afterwards, his eyes were put out, as a
punishment for his treachery. The entrance was then
covered over and Newgrange was forgotten until 1699,
when a team of roadbuilders happened upon it.

KNOWTH PASSAGE TOMB, KERB STONES, CO. MEATH

Above: ALTHOUGH ITS FAME has always been overshadowed by
Newgrange, the tomb of Knowth is scarcely less remarkable. The
eastern tomb terminates in a cruciform chamber with three niches.
Around the main cairn, there are more than a dozen smaller mounds,
each containing their own passage-grave. Much later, a network of
souterrains was also constructed within the Knowth complex.

KNOWTH PASSAGE TOMB, KERB STONES, CO. MEATH

Above: THE SECRETS OF KNOWTH remained hidden for much longer than those of Newgrange. Its central cairn contains an arrangement of two passage-graves, constructed back-to-back and oriented towards the spring and autumn equinoxes. Inside, the stones are decorated with an array of circular and spiral grooves. The designs here come from a stone basin in the eastern tomb, which was used in ancient cremation rites.

Broken Cross & Sundial, Kells, Co. Meath

THIS SITE OWES ITS FAME to the lavish illuminated manuscript, *The Book of Kells*, which was housed here for many centuries. The monastery itself was founded in the early years of the 9th century as a sanctuary for the monks of Iona, who had been driven out of their home by Norse raiders. Construction work was completed by 814, when Kells became head of the Columban federation of monasteries, the order following the teachings of St Columba. Mindful of the destruction threatened by the Vikings, many abbots commissioned stone crosses and sculpture as lasting memorials to their faith. At Kells, there are remains of five 10th-century crosses. The Broken Cross (right), would have been particularly imposing, reaching a height of around 6 metres (20 feet) and boasting a fine display of Biblical scenes. Here, the Fall is depicted. Adam and Eve are framed by the branches of the Tree of Knowledge while in the centre, the serpent coils round its trunk. Part of an early sundial has also survived (left). This would have been a common sight at many early churches, since it provided worshippers with their only reliable means of attending services on time.

DUNDALK, CO. LOUTH

Right: THIS 12TH-CENTURY motte and bailey were built by Bertram de Verdon, an Anglo-Norman lord, to protect his property in the surrounding countryside. There are suggestions, however, that the castle was constructed over a prehistoric ringfort. If so, it may well be the Dún Dealgan (Dealga's Fort), which gave Dundalk its name and which plays such a prominent role in Irish legend – for this was the birthplace and home of Cú Chulainn, the greatest of the ancient warrior heroes. In the *Cattle Raid of Cooley*, the most famous of the pre-Christian epics, Cú Chulainn used Dealga's Fort as his base when defending Ulster against the invading armies of Connaught. By day, he would challenge their champions to single combat, and by night, he would hurl down slingshots on the enemy camp. Such was the ferocity of these attacks that, it was said, no living man or beast dared to show their face between Dealga and the sea.

MUIREDACH'S CROSS, MONASTERBOICE, CO. LOUTH

Left: THIS IS ONE OF THE MOST ORNATE of the later Celtic crosses. An inscription on the base invites the reader to 'pray for Muiredach, by whom this cross was made'. Almost certainly, this refers to the important local figure who was abbot of Monasterboice from 887 until his death in 923, and who also held the post of vice-abbot of Armagh. The biblical scenes portrayed on the monument served a practical, didactic purpose, as crosses of this kind were often the focus of open-air prayer meetings. For example, Doubting Thomas and the Arrest of Christ appear here on the shaft, while the Crucifixion is depicted within the wheel. Masons also liked to add lighthearted touches. The image of the beard-tuggers (right), which is featured on the side of the cross, was borrowed from contemporary manuscripts. There, the bodies of the men would be flattened out into ribbon-like forms and used in interlacing patterns. The length of the beards could be prodigious, and arms, legs and hair could also be interwoven. Monasterboice is on a ley line, which also takes in Tara and Knowth.

HILL OF SLANE, CO. MEATH

Left: THE REMAINS OF A 16th-century friary now stand on the site where, by tradition, St Patrick first threw down the gauntlet to the forces of paganism. On Easter Saturday in 432, there was a heathen festival at nearby Tara. At its climax, when the druids were due to light a ceremonial bonfire, Patrick pre-empted them by kindling his own fire on the Hill of Slane. The druids and the high king were horrified at this, for it fulfilled a longstanding prophecy that the keeper of a rival flame would come to Tara and eclipse their power for ever.

TRIM CASTLE & THE ROUND TOWER, KELLS, CO. MEATH

Left: INITIALLY, ROUND TOWERS in early Ireland were simple belltowers, calling the monks into prayer from their work in the fields. During the Viking period, however, they proved invaluable as look-out posts and treasure stores. This accounts for their high entrance points and for the fact that they were built out of stone, rather than timber. The monks of Kells had good reason for constructing such a tower, as their monastery was looted no fewer than six times in the 10th century.

Right: TRIM'S RISE TO prominence followed the success of a preacher named Loman, who converted the local chieftain and was granted land to build a church. By tradition, this achievement was intimately connected with St Patrick's mission, for the chieftain in question was Feidlimid, the son of Loegaire of Tara, while Loman was the saint's nephew. Later, Trim assumed great strategic importance and its castle became one of the principal strongholds of the English Pale. Doubts have been raised about its defensive capabilities, but it was deemed secure enough to host several Anglo-Norman parliaments.

MELLIFONT ABBEY, CO. LOUTH

Right: MELLIFONT ABBEY, CO. LOUTH, was the first Cistercian house to be built in Ireland. It was the brainchild of St Malachy, a reforming cleric and former archbishop of Armagh, who founded it in 1142 on land donated by a local chieftain, Donagh O'Carroll. Further financial support came from King Muirchertach Mac Loughlainn, who endowed the abbey with 160 cows and 1.7 kg (60 ounces) of gold. Malachy was inspired by his meetings with the leader of the Cistercian order, St Bernard of Clairvaux, who sent an architect named Robert to supervise the project.

The finished buildings – remarkable though they must have been – were close to English and Continental models, signalling the decline of native Irish styles. Among the surviving features are a pseudo-crypt, designed to prevent flooding from the river; part of the octagonal lavabo, where the monks used to wash themselves in a fountain; and the delicate encaustic tiles from the abbey church now set into the floor of the 14th-century chapter-house (below). After its suppression in 1539 Mellifont was turned into a stronghold; William of Orange used it as his base during the Battle of the Boyne.

THE KINGDOM OF
MUNSTER

THE ANCIENT NAME for Munster was Mumu or Mumhan, thought to derive from the name of an early ruler, King Eocho Mumho. In common with Ulster and Leinster, the suffix '-ster' is of Viking origin. Legend describes it as a place of mystery, connected with the Otherworld. The sinister gathering place of the dead, Tech Duinn (House of Donn, the god of death) was supposedly situated on an island close to Munster's shores.

The first identifiable tribes belonged to the Erainn people, who were led by the petty kings of west Kerry. From an early point in the historic period, however, the dominant force in the area was the Eoghanacht dynasty. Very little is known about Eoghan, the founder of the clan, although some of

LEFT CRAGGAUNOWEN, CO. CLARE

Reconstruction of a crannóg, a fortified lake-dwelling. This constitutes part of the 'Living Past' project, set up in the grounds of Craggaunowen Castle.

LEFT POULNABRONE, CO. CLARE

The prehistoric tomb of Poulnabrone, a portal dolmen set on the Burren's spectacular limestone plateau. The Burren takes its name from boireann, a Gaelic word for 'rocky land'.

According to the annals, the Eoghanacht established themselves at Cashel (see p. 139) during the reign of Oenghus. He became king there in the mid-5th century, with both pagan and Christian sources claiming the credit for his success. The former attributed his victories to the support of a druid named Boinda while, in the *Tripartite Life of St Patrick*, it was the king's decision to become baptized which was deemed crucial.

There is no firm proof that St Patrick himself ever came to Cashel, but the traditional links with the place are of great antiquity, and the towering base of the fortress has long been known as St Patrick's Rock. In addition, the meagre information that is available on the missions in Ireland before the arrival of St Patrick suggests that their efforts were concentrated in the south. In Munster, the leading figure was St Ailbe. Virtually nothing is known about the saint, apart from a series of colourful legends. According to these, he was suckled by a she-wolf and eventually retired to the fabled Land of Promise, a variant of the Celtic Otherworld.

In reality, his two main achievements were the foundation of a church at Emly – the most important Christian site in Munster, before the rise of Cashel – and the procurement of land on the Aran Isles from King Oenghus, where St Enda established his monastery.

the annalists relate that his real name was Mug Nuadat, and that he and another leader divided Ireland between them; southern Ireland was popularly known as Mug's Half.

A more popular myth attributed the success of the Eoghanacht to Conall Corc, one of Eoghan's descendants. He had a British mother and returned to Ireland, so it was said, after a period of exile in 'Pictland'. The latter may refer to Wales rather than Scotland however, for it is known that a group of Irish settlers was expelled from the Welsh coast in *c.* 400 AD. Conall's initial power base was small, but his people managed to extend their influence rapidly, mainly through judicious alliances with certain Erainn tribes and the dwindling power of the Laigin tribe in neighbouring Leinster.

Throughout the early Christian period, Munster became a favourite destination for those holy men who wished to lead the solitary life. The most famous of their settlements can be seen on the tiny island of Great Skellig, probably begun by St Finan in the 7th century. The province also has strong associations with St Brendan (484–577), one of the most renowned of all the Irish monks. He founded a monastery at Ardfert and is also linked with a reclusive site on Brandon Mountain, in the Dingle peninsula (see p. 122).

Cashel, meanwhile, remained the political focus. For much of the early historic era there was intense rivalry between branches of the Eoghanacht for the title of king. In this sense, Cashel was the southern equivalent of Tara, the seat of the high kings. Despite these inter-tribal squabbles Munster was probably the most peaceful of the Irish provinces. Comparatively few of its ancient rulers met with a violent death, and there are signs that it developed the most sophisticated culture. Plentiful inscriptions in ogham, an ancient form of writing, confirm a flourishing aristocratic caste, and the earliest written examples of Irish poetry were produced here in the late 6th century. Some argue that Munster's contacts with Gaul helped to maintain its superiority in this field.

Many of these advances were swept away when Munster fell prey to Viking marauders. Their first attack took place in 795, and for more than a century southern Ireland suffered greatly at their hands. Effective resistance did not arrive until the Eoghanacht were supplanted by a new dynasty, the Dál Chais. Led by two brothers, Mahon and Brian Boru, these people took Cashel in 963 and inflicted a crushing defeat on the Norsemen at Sollohod. Brian Boru went on to even greater fame, winning another decisive victory at Clontarf in 1014. This proved a major turning point in the struggle against the Vikings, although it cost Brian Boru his life.

With the onset of the Middle Ages, the political geography of Munster changed. In place of the rivalry between east and west, the principal divisions were now between Thomond (the north-west) and Desmond (the south). Here, the leading families were, respectively, the O'Briens and the Mac Carthys. The former were the successors of Brian Boru, while the latter were the descendants of the Eoghanacht.

LEFT LEAMANEH CASTLE, CO. CLARE

Leamaneh Castle was built in 1643 by Conor O'Brien, a descendant of Brian Boru. Conor's wife was Máire Rua (Red Mary), who, according to one story, offered to marry any Cromwellian officer in order to prevent its confiscation.

OGHAM STONE, MAUMANORIG ENCLOSURE, CO. KERRY

Below: THE ANCIENT OGHAM alphabet takes its name from Ogma, the Celtic god of eloquence. Individual letters were composed of straight or slanting lines, notched onto the edges of stones and pillars. The system appears to have originated in south-west Ireland, reaching the peak of its popularity in the 5th and 6th centuries. Since this coincided precisely with the early Christian missions, it is not surprising that many of the stones were Christianized with the addition of a cross.

STAIGUE FORT, CO. KERRY

Right: SITUATED IN A commanding position in the Ring of Kerry, Staigue is one of the most impressive prehistoric hillforts in the country. Its internal diameter is 23.8 metres (78 feet) wide, and the surviving walls rise to a height of 5.2 metres (17 feet) in places. Although its main purpose would have been defense, there is a theory that Staigue Fort was sometimes used as a refuge for pilgrims travelling to Skellig Michael, a small island near the west coast which is visible from the fort.

Staigue Fort, Co. Kerry

Right: STAIGUE'S EXCELLENT STATE of preservation offers intriguing evidence about the purpose and construction of ancient ringforts. Its walls are 3.9 metres (13 feet) thick and they incline slightly inwards, making life more difficult for potential attackers. Access to the upper parts of the wall could be gained through a system of internal stairways. In addition, two small passages set into the walls would have offered the same kind of protection as a souterrain (see p. 62). There has been much debate as to whether ringforts were genuine military structures or simply fortified farmsteads, capable only of keeping out wolves and petty thieves, but Staigue Fort was certainly the former.

RINGFORT, CAHERDORGAN NORTH, CO. KERRY

Above: THE DWELLING-PLACES inside individual ringforts varied
according to the wealth of their occupants. Some were simple
post-and-wattle buildings, while others were sturdier, drystone huts.
The latter were particularly popular in western Ireland, as the
remains at Caherdorgan confirm. Huts of this kind were not
always fully corbelled, occasionally some had a roof of thatch
supported by a wooden post.

ENTRANCE, DUNBEG FORT, CO. KERRY

Above: BECAUSE PROMONTORY forts were virtually surrounded by the sea, they offered a considerable degree of protection to their inhabitants. Even so, the builders of Dunbeg Fort took no chances; a series of banks and ditches, together with a thick stone rampart, was erected in front of a single beehive hut. In addition, a souterrain linked the rampart with the first row of ditches, therefore increasing the fort's protection.

UPPER LAKE, KILLARNEY, CO. KERRY

Right: THE WIND WHIPS UP around the shores of
Killarney's lakes, evoking memories of the fairy people
from the *sidhe*. Superstitious folk used to believe that the
old gods travelled in the breeze so they blessed
themselves whenever they saw a gust of wind whirling
the leaves on a country path or shaking the reeds at the
water's edge. Magic of another kind went on beneath the
surface of the lake, where a chieftain called O'Donoghue
held court, emerging each year at the festival of Beltane,
a Celtic fire festival celebrated on May 1st.

An Ráth, Co. Clare

Left: A RATH IS A TYPE of ringfort, formed out of earthen ramparts rather than a stone wall. Enclosures might be round, oval or pear-shaped, and the average diameter is around 30 metres (100 feet). Most raths have a single, circular rampart, though this example has two, separated by a ditch. In some cases, the central area was also heightened to form an artificial platform or mound. For obvious reasons, raths were most common in areas where stone was in short supply. They are often hard to detect, as the invading Anglo-Normans transformed many of them into mottes, the artificial hills on which castles were placed.

Bantry Bay, Co. Cork

Left: ONE OF THE MOST arresting panoramic vistas of ancient Ireland, Bantry was the traditional departure point for Brendan the Navigator's voyages in the Atlantic. Ostensibly, he was following the example of other Irish monks, who used to venture out in their coracles looking for their 'desert in the ocean' where they could lead a penitential existence. According to legend, Brendan's voyages took him to a number of fabulous destinations, before he eventually found his 'Land of Promise', and returned home content. Some believe that this was a reference to the Canaries, while others have speculated about a pre-Viking voyage to America.

STONE CIRCLE, LOUGH GUR, CO. LIMERICK

Right: SITUATED AROUND THE shores of Lough Gur is the
richest concentration of prehistoric sites in Ireland. The
great stone circle, said to be the largest in the country, is
50 metres (150 feet) in diameter and is ringed with
earthworks that are 10 metres (30 feet) wide. It has a
paved entry passage, flanked by portal stones, and the
centre of the circle has been raised with a level of clay.
Other finds in the area include a group of neolithic huts,
some smaller stone circles, several cashels and graves,
and a crannóg, an ancient Celtic lake dwelling.

FAHAN BEEHIVE HUTS, DINGLE PENINSULA, CO. KERRY

BECAUSE OF THE abundance of rocks in the area, beehive huts were extremely common in south-western Ireland. More than 400 have been discovered in the Dingle peninsula alone, the best of these being in the 'village' of Fahan. The rows of stones were probably covered with clods of earth to offer some additional protection against the elements, and entrances were usually kept as small as possible. Beehive huts are hard to date, but they seem to have been most popular during the early Christian era.

Quin Friary, Co. Clare

Left: MANY RELIGIOUS HOUSES were built on earlier Christian foundations, but Quin's Franciscan friary has the rare distinction of incorporating a secular site. This was the Norman stronghold of Thomas de Clare, the lord of Thomond, which had been pillaged in 1286. The castle lay in ruins for 150 years until it was granted to the friars by the Macnamaras in the 1430s. There are claims that Quin became the first Observantine house in Ireland, following the austere lifestyle led by their founder St Francis.

ADARE CASTLE, CO. LIMERICK

Right: SET PICTURESQUELY ON the banks of the river
Maigue, Adare Castle provides a telling example of
Norman feudal strength. Within a decade or so of their
arrival on Irish soil in the 1170s, the Anglo-Norman
adventurers began to cement their power by erecting a
series of impressive strongholds. Although the precise
details of its origin are unknown, Adare Castle probably
dates from the 1220s. It may have been built by the
O'Donovans or perhaps by Geoffrey de Marisco, who
owned a manor house there. Either way, Adare Castle is
now more closely associated with the earls of Desmond,
who held it in the 16th century.

SHEILA-NA-GIG, KILLINABOY, CO. CLARE

Below: THE RUINED CHURCH at Killinaboy stands on the site of an ancient monastery, dedicated to St Inghean Bhaoth. Its most surprising feature is a tiny sheila-na-gig, fixed above the south door. The presence of this Irish fertility goddess, blatantly displaying her sexuality, provides clear evidence of the Church's willingness to placate its heathen rivals.

GALLARUS ORATORY, CO. KERRY

Right: WITH ITS DISTINCTIVE, boat-shaped appearance, Gallurus is certainly the most famous of the early Christian oratories. Its construction utilized the drystone roofing technique known as corbelling that had been pioneered by neolithic tomb-builders. The walls are 0.9 metres (3 feet) thick and the only concession to luxury is a tiny window, cut out of a single stone.

Rahinnane Castle, Co. Kerry

Right: RAHINNANE CASTLE WAS built on the foundations of an ancient ringfort and souterrain. Its stumpy remains appear very battle-worn, which is apt, since one of the warrior-hero Finn Mac Cool's greatest victories took place at nearby Ventry. With typical gusto, the chronicler of these legendary feats told how the elements themselves reflected the conflict:

The earth trembled in foreboding at the terrible slaughter; the sun veiled itself in darkness before the clamour of the grey hosts; and the ravens, the wolf-packs, and the wild women of the glen shrieked together like demons, urging the warriors on in their bloody fray…

THE CLIFFS OF MOHER, CO. CLARE

Left: RISING TO A HEIGHT OF over 200 metres (650 feet)
and extending for more than 8 kilometres (5 miles), the
Cliffs of Moher form one of the most dramatic stretches
of Ireland's coastline. The cliffs take their name from an
ancient promontory fort called Mothair, which must
have been almost impregnable, until it was removed a
century ago to make way for a signalling tower. Not far
away is St Brigid's Well, which used to be the focus of
great celebrations at Lughnasadh, the Celtic summer
festival, while further down the coast the legendary city
of Cill Stuihín is said to lie submerged.

ROMANESQUE DOORWAY, DYSERT O'DEA, CO. CLARE

Left: DYSERT TAKES ITS NAME from the *dísert* or 'hermitage' of St Tola (d. 737), who also founded a church at Clonard. The church was restored in 1683 by Michael O'Dea, a descendant of the original landowners. Among other things, O'Dea reassembled this romanesque arch (detail, right), incorporating some of the stonework from the neighbouring church of Rath. Dysert was also the scene of an important battle in 1318, when Irish forces defeated Richard de Clare, thereby halting the Anglo-Norman advance into Thomond.

Abbey Ruins, Cashel, Co. Tipperary

Right: CASHEL IS SURROUNDED by castles and here, within sight of St Patrick's rock, can be found the ruins of Hore Abbey, a 13th-century Cistercian foundation. Previously, there had been a Benedictine priory on this site, but Archbishop Dáibhí Mac Cearbhaill expelled the monks after dreaming that they were hatching a plot to behead him. Close by, there are also the remains of a Dominican friary. Known as St Dominic's Priory, this was founded in 1243 by Archbishop Mac Ceallaigh.

ROCK OF CASHEL, CO. TIPPERARY

Left: THE SILHOUETTE OF THE buildings on the Rock of
Cashel, also known as St Patrick's Rock, is one of the
most familiar sights in Ireland. Part fortress, part palace
and part church, Cashel belonged initially to the
Eoghanacht dynasty, the powerful kings who ruled over
the southern half of Ireland. Here, St Patrick converted
and baptized King Oenghus. During the ceremony, it is
said that he impaled the king's foot with the sharp point
of his crozier, but Oenghus bore this with fortitude,
believing it to be part of the ritual. Cashel acquired its
ecclesiastical character in 1101, when Muircheartach
O'Brien, ruler of Cashel, bestowed it on the Church,
expecting it to become the new see of Munster.

THE KINGDOM OF
LEINSTER

THE PROVINCE of Leinster used to be called Laigin, which was also the name of its ancient people. The source of this word is uncertain, although it is said to derive from the *laighne*, or spears, of the Gaulish warriors who lent assistance to Móen, a legendary prince of Leinster. Prince Móen had suffered cruel treatment at the hands of his uncle Cobhthach, who had killed the king and forced young Móen to eat his heart. However, the prince escaped to Gaul where he befriended a king of the Fir Morca people, who helped him regain his throne.

Early historical accounts suggest that the kingdom of Leinster was occupied by three waves of invaders, namely the Fir Domnann, the Gáileóin and the

LEFT: ST PATRICK'S CATHEDRAL, DUBLIN

The Choir Banners, symbolic swords and helmets of the Order of St Patrick. The saint is said to have called forth a well and baptized new converts on this site.

Laigin. The Fir Domnann were probably the first to arrive. They conquered large tracts of Ireland, leaving their mark on a number of place-names, such as Irrus Domnann (now Erris). They were succeeded by the Gáileóin, who may have been a race of British mercenaries, and finally the Laigin. The origins of the latter are disputed, although it is possible that they came from the Lleyn peninsula in north Wales. In any event, they were the only invaders to survive into the historic period.

Prior to this, Leinster was associated with the legend of Finn Mac Cool, Ireland's legendary warrior-hero. Finn's stronghold was at the Hill of Allen (Almain), a few miles from Kildare. Archaeologists believe that this may have been the site of a prehistoric tumulus, which could explain why early storytellers chose to link the place with a legendary character. The hill was surrounded by dense bogland – on some 18th-century maps it was described as the Isle of Allen – and this ties in well with the ancient tales of Finn, which describe his homeland as a remote, marshy wilderness.

In the course of his adventures Finn travelled to the sacred site of Tara, where he enlisted in the service of the high king, Cormac Mac Art, and took command of his royal bodyguard, known as the Fianna. Finn's exploits with this noble body of knights are often reminiscent of the deeds of King Arthur. Indeed, in the episode of Diarmaid and Gráinne (see pp. 20–21, 86–87) there is even a striking parallel with the inconstancy of Queen Guinevere.

At the same time, Leinster's fabled involvement with Tara echoes the province's historical development. The Laigin's principal neighbours were the Osraige (deer-people) to the west and Meath to the north. In time, the Osraige tribe formed the kingdom of Ossory, which acted as a convenient buffer-zone between Leinster and Munster. Instead the Laigin chiefs turned their attention towards the north, competing with the southern Uí Néill tribe for the possession of Tara. This bitter rivalry lasted until the arrival of the Vikings, resulting, more often than not, in defeat for the Laigin.

LEFT: JERPOINT ABBEY, CO. KILKENNY

This 16th-century tomb portrays three of the apostles with their attributes. St Peter holds a key, St Andrew is shown with a saltire cross, and St James bears a scallop shell and staff, the traditional symbols of a pilgrim.

The best-documented of the early conflicts concerned Loegaire, the high king who clashed with St Patrick on the Hill of Slane (see pp. 98–99). He triumphed over the Laigin in 452 and 453, but was defeated at the battle of Ath Dara five years later. When he died his people obeyed his wishes and buried him in an upright position, facing his enemy to the south. Loegaire's defeat, however, proved to be just a temporary setback for the Uí Néill. Resounding victories at Croghan Hill (475), Teltown (494) and Druim Derge (516) turned the tide, penning the Laigin back into the south-east corner of the country for generations to come.

During the early Christian period Leinster figured prominently in the spread of the monastic movement. In Clonmacnois, Glendalough and Durrow, it possessed three of the most influential foundations of the time. It could also boast of having Ireland's second most famous saint after St Patrick; this was St Brigid (c. 450–c. 523), the abbess of Kildare, who had earned the nickname 'Mary of the Gaels' after receiving a vision of the Virgin. Details of her life are shadowy, and early accounts suggest that she became associated with the pagan traditions of a Celtic goddess, also called Brigid. The saint's feast-day was celebrated on February 1st, the same day as the festival of Imbolc, dedicated to the goddess. Equally, there were

LEFT: BROWNESHILL DOLMEN, CO. CARLOW

The tightly wedged supporting stones failed to prevent Browneshill's gigantic capstone from slipping backwards. Estimated at 100 tons, it is by far the heaviest in Ireland.

certainly pagan overtones in the perpetual fire that was tended at Kildare, set in a circular enclosure which was forbidden to all men.

Kildare was sacked by the Vikings in 835, a fate that was shared by many other churches in Leinster. It seems that the province suffered greater devastation than its neighbours, and it was here that the raiders first attempted to create permanent settlements. Dublin, Waterford and Wexford all owe their origins to this policy. In the case of Dublin, the process began in 841 when the Norsemen constructed their first homesteads by the river Liffey. Norse reinforcements arrived a decade later and by 871 the tiny kingdom of Dublinshire was firmly established as a base for trading and making inland raids.

The attitude of the Leinster kings towards these foreign settlements was equivocal. Occasionally, Leinster and Dublin formed alliances in order to challenge the growing strength of Munster. However these pacts were overturned when the Munster leader, Brian Boru, embarked upon his triumphant campaigns against the invaders, which culminated in the decisive victory at Clontarf in 1014.

PUNCHESTOWN STANDING STONE, CO. KILDARE

Left: THERE HAS BEEN a great deal of speculation about the purpose of single standing stones. Some people believe that they were erected at the burial sites of ancient chieftains; others that they were designed to mark territorial boundaries or major routes. There is even a theory that they were meant to help cattle scratch themselves. In the case of the Punchestown monolith, this question was answered in 1934, when the stone was repositioned and a cist (a chest-like tomb) was revealed. Its occupant must surely have been important, for the 7-metre (23-foot) monument is the tallest in Ireland.

BROWNESHILL DOLMEN, CO. CARLOW

Right: PORTAL DOLMENS ARE perhaps the most impressive of the megalithic chamber tombs. It required considerable technical skill and manpower to transport the stones using a system of rollers and then to arrange them in such precarious formations. Nowhere would these problems have been more evident than at Browneshill, where the mighty capstone weighs 101,600 kg (100 tons), easily the heaviest example in Ireland. As a result, two of the supporting uprights have collapsed and the rear section now slopes down to the ground.

DUNBRODY ABBEY, CO. WEXFORD

Right: THE IMPOSING RUINS of Dunbrody Abbey are a
testament to the growth of foreign influences in
Ireland. The land was donated in 1178 by Hervey de
Montmorency, the uncle and seneschal of Strongbow,
the best-known of the Anglo-Norman adventurers. The
original recipient was a Cistercian abbey in Shropshire,
which rapidly passed on the gift to St Mary's Abbey in
Dublin, after hearing reports about the barrenness of
the land and the 'wildness and ferocity of the local
barbarians'. Unwittingly, Hervey may have helped to
reinforce this image by stipulating that outlaws were to
be granted asylum at his church. As a result, it soon
earned the nickname of St Mary of Refuge. Most of the
abbey was constructed in the early years of the 13th
century, in the austere style that was typical of
continental, Cistercian architecture.

OGHAM STONE, ARDMORE CHURCH, CO. WATERFORD

Left: OGHAM WAS THE earliest form of writing known in Ireland. The druids employed it for incantations, and some inscriptions have survived on tomb-markers. Because of their heathen associations, however, such stones were usually destroyed or Christianized by missionaries – and this is what happened here. The original inscription is thought to refer to 'Lugaid, descendant of Nia Segamain', one of the early pagan kings, but at a later stage, a suffragan bishop named Dolatus had his own name added, thereby conferring upon the stone an air of Christian respectability.

ARDMORE CHURCH, CO. WATERFORD

Right: ARDMORE'S REMARKABLE church was founded by St Declan, one of the four 5th-century missionaries said to have preached in Ireland before the arrival of St Patrick. According to a local tradition, Declan's handbell and vestments floated across the Irish Sea on a boulder, which came to rest on Ardmore's beach. Among the subjects portrayed are the Fall, the Judgment of Solomon, and the Adoration of the Magi.

'WEEPERS', JERPOINT ABBEY, CO. KILKENNY

Left: THE CISTERCIAN ABBEY of Jerpoint was founded in the mid-12th century by Donal Mac Gillapatrick, King of Ossary. It was substantially rebuilt in the 15th century, and its chief glory lies not so much in its architecture as in its carvings. These include a fine series of statues in the cloister, along with some remarkable tomb-sculpture.

Shown here are three figures known as 'weepers', so-called because of their association with tombs. This particular tomb was executed by Rory O'Tunney, and features the Apostles St Thomas, St Bartholomew and St Philip. The first two carry the symbols of their martyrdom – a spear and a knife used for flaying skin – while Philip holds the loaves that he helped to distribute at the Feeding of the Five Thousand.

DETAIL FROM THE MOONE CROSS, CO. WATERFORD

Above: MOONE BELONGED to the Columban group of monasteries founded in the 6th century. Accordingly, its high cross was dedicated to the saint and some aspects of its decoration were inspired by Columban manuscripts. These intertwined creatures, for example, might easily have sprung from the pages of the *Book of Kells*. Two leonine beasts stand back-to-back, sharing a single pair of hind legs, while a series of serpentine monsters sprout from their flanks and attack them.

DETAIL FROM THE MOONE CROSS, CO. WATERFORD

Above: UNUSUALLY, THE CROSS at Moone was carved from granite, an unyielding material that forced certain economies of style upon the artist. As a result, the figures display a certain simplicity, with their squat bodies and childlike faces. Here, the Sacrifice of Isaac is depicted – Abraham raises the knife, as his son bends over the sacrificial altar. Above them is the ram, which will be eventually killed in Isaac's place. The theme was popular as it prefigured Christ's sacrifice at the Crucifixion.

GLENDALOUGH, CO. WICKLOW

Left: THIS SPECTACULAR MONASTERY was founded in the 6th century by St Kevin, a member of the ruling Leinster dynasty, who chose instead to become a hermit. His original retreat was in a barely accessible cave, known today as St Kevin's Bed. As his fame increased, other structures were added in a haphazard fashion. The present jumble of buildings, which is more akin to a tiny village than to the traditional idea of a monastery, offers a telling picture of early monastic life. In keeping with the beauty of the place, Kevin's miracles were closely linked with nature. Once, when he was ill, an otter brought him a salmon to eat in his cave. On another occasion, so the legend goes, a blackbird laid an egg in his outstretched hand. Not wishing to disturb it, the saint stayed rooted to the spot until it hatched out. These gentle tales may be misleading, however, for the area was far from tranquil. As the lofty Round Tower suggests, Glendalough was a popular target for Viking raiders and was looted on at least four occasions.

BURIAL GROUND, GLENDALOUGH MONASTERY, CO. WICKLOW

Below: THE PRECINCTS OF THE monastery contain a wide scattering of early grave-slabs and crosses. Many of them are inscribed with the word '*oroit*', from the Latin 'to pray'. Not all of the graves belong to monks, for Glendalough also became the resting place of the local overlords, the Uí Dúnlainge. This honour was doubtless a reflection of St Kevin's fame. Even so, it is ironic that a monastery, which was deliberately located in a remote and isolated spot, should have effectively been used as a royal chapel.

ST KEVIN'S KITCHEN, GLENDALOUGH, CO. WICKLOW

Right: THIS STRANGE, ROMANESQUE building was probably designed as an oratory or a mortuary chapel. Its curious nickname may be due to its chimney-like turret. Alternatively, it may be a distant echo of ancient pagan traditions about a sacred hearth-flame. This was supposed to be a perpetual fire, which provided heat for all the other hearths in the community. Christian settlements were often built upon earlier sanctuaries, where the hearth-stone would be broken up and incorporated into the new structure.

CASTLE OF JOHN DE GREY, CLONMACNOIS, CO. OFFALY

Right: ON A GRASSY MOUND near the banks of the river Shannon, a cluster of stone fragments balance precariously, like a row of tumbling dice. This is all that remains of the castle erected in 1212 by John de Grey, the Bishop of Norwich. Its construction dates from the period when King John (1199–1216) was seeking to consolidate his power in Ireland. Accordingly, in 1208, he appointed one of his most able administrators as his Justiciar (chief representative). De Grey had been John's nominee for the post of Archbishop of Canterbury, and he soon demonstrated his efficiency by building a series of powerful strongholds, most notably at Athlone and Clonmacnois. The latter remained largely intact until the 17th century, when it was destroyed by Cromwellians.